LICENSE AGREEMENT

This book (the "Book") is a product provided by RC PRESS o/b AirsoftPRESS (being referred to as "RCPRESS" in this document). You may not modify the Book or create any derivative work of the Book or its accompanying documentation. Derivative works include but are not limited to translations. You may not copy any part of the Book unless formal written authorization is obtained from us. RCPRESS will not be held liable for any advice or suggestions given in this book. If the reader wants to follow a suggestion, it is at his or her own discretion. Suggestions are only offered to help.

Table of Contents

This book has been updated in April 2022.

ABOUT THIS BOOK

This training book has been developed from the ground up for beginners who know little about electric power RC technology. As part of our RC Technology Self-Paced Training Series, this book gives an introduction to the modern EP offroad architecture. The primary goal of this book is to explain the various technical concepts in very simple language.

We believe that this book and its support materials have everything you need for an informative, interesting, challenging and entertaining RC educational experience.

As you read this book, if you have questions, send an e-mail to editor@rcpress.com; we will respond promptly. You are encouraged to visit our Web site, www.rcpress.com, regularly. We use the Web site to keep our readers and industry clients informed of the latest news on RCPRESS publications and services. Please also check the Web site occasionally for errata.

BASIC CONCEPT OF OFFROAD RC CARS

Offroad buggies are primarily designed for speed and jumps. Bashing is never desired. To achieve proper speed the body must be slim (so it can be less heavy). To jump and land safely the entire structure must be strong and flexible enough (so it won't break).

Unlike those trucks with big wheels, buggies are in fact NOT too suitable to run on grassland. The buggy tires are not big enough to provide enough grip on thick grasses. Stadium Trucks are primarily designed for jumps and off-road racing, while Short Course Trucks are made to be extremely durable (to absorb contact from other vehicles better than traditional RC trucks) for frequent bashing. Their design concepts are totally different.

BODY PROTECTION

Large front and rear foam bumpers can offer sufficient protection when unexpected bashing takes place. HOWEVER, larger bumpers are heavier and can affect the weight balance during and after a jump. **For buggies, small bumpers are usually more preferable.**

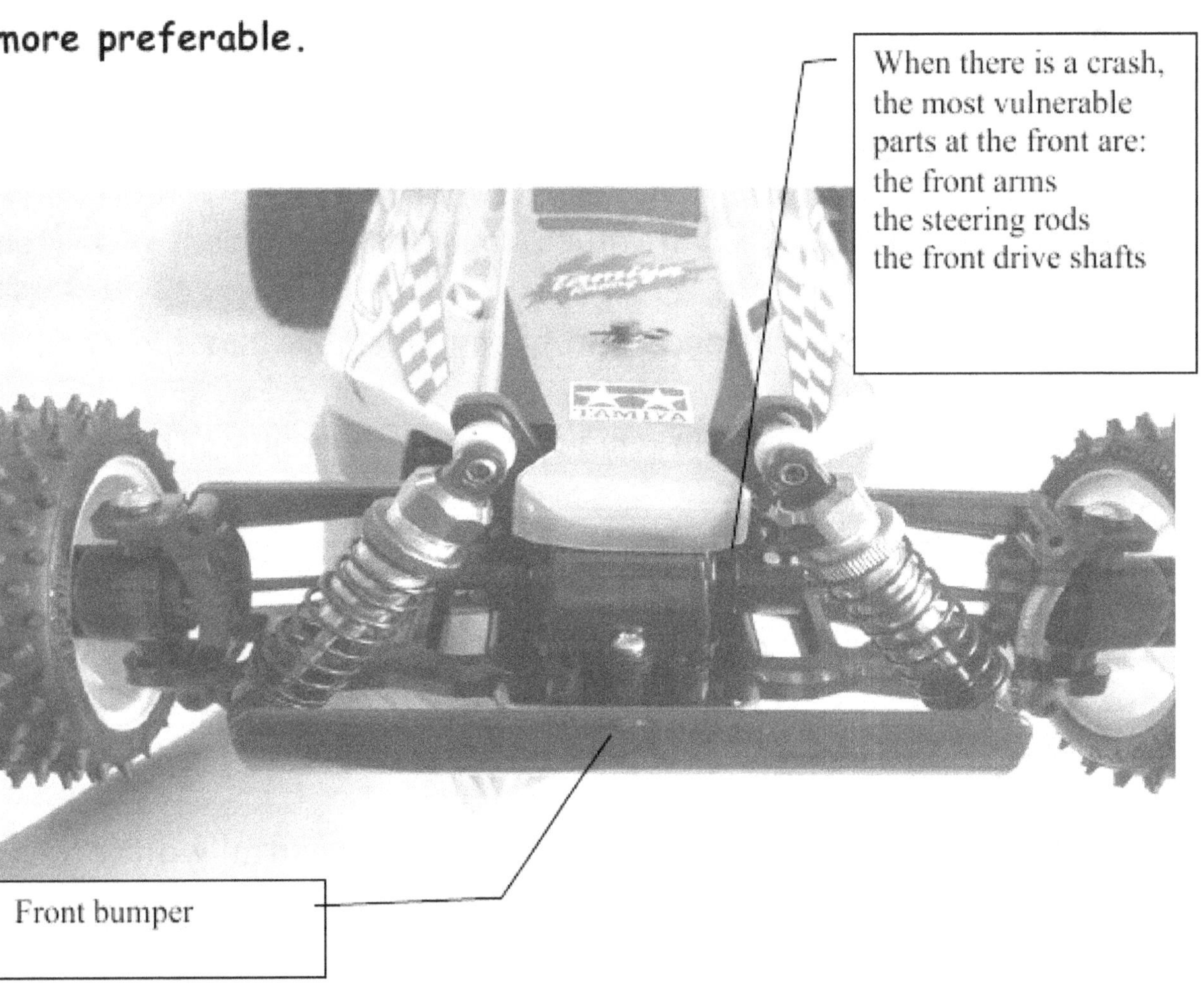

Front bumper

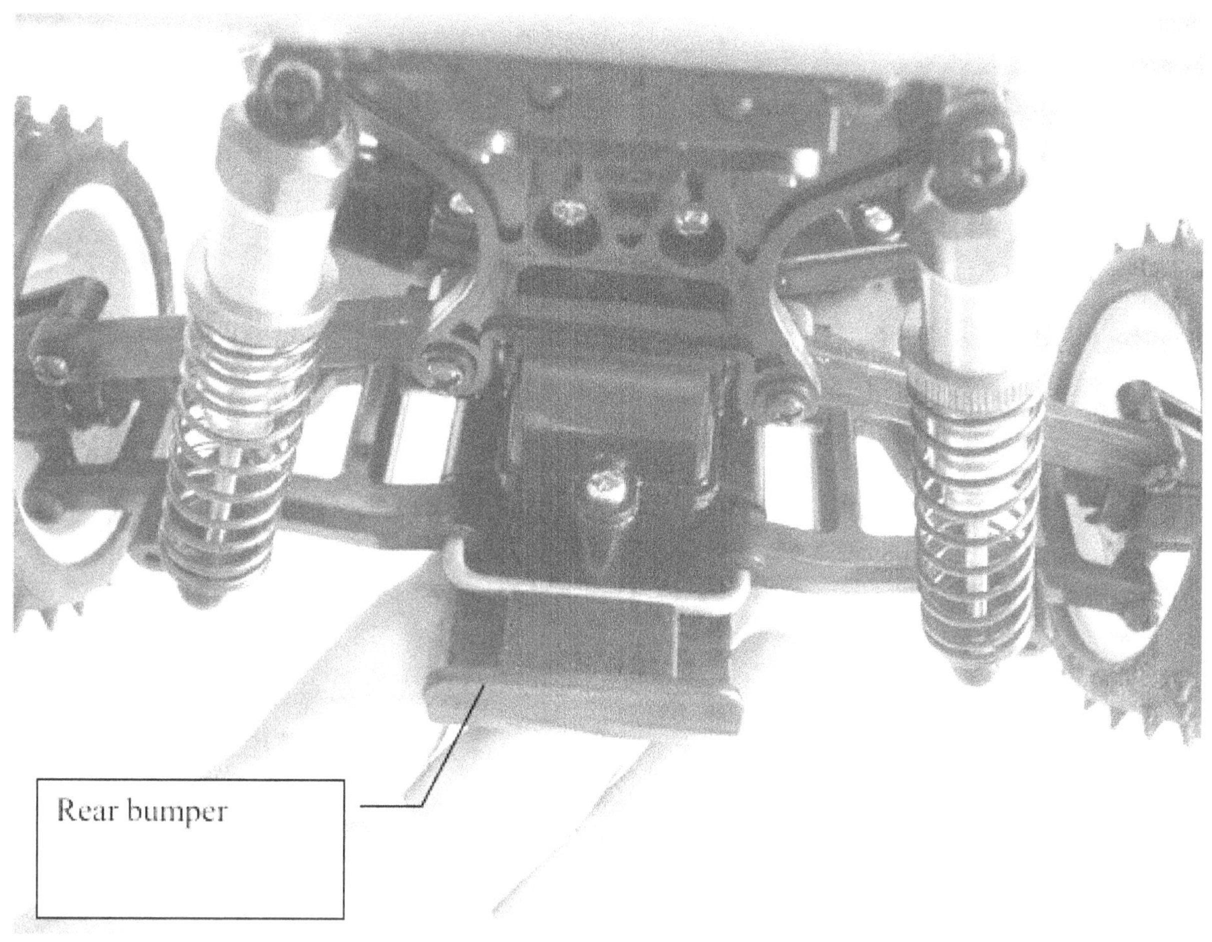

Our demo buggy has a wide front bumper out of the box which can protect most of the front arm assemblies. It also has a metal rod reinforcement to offer additional strength.

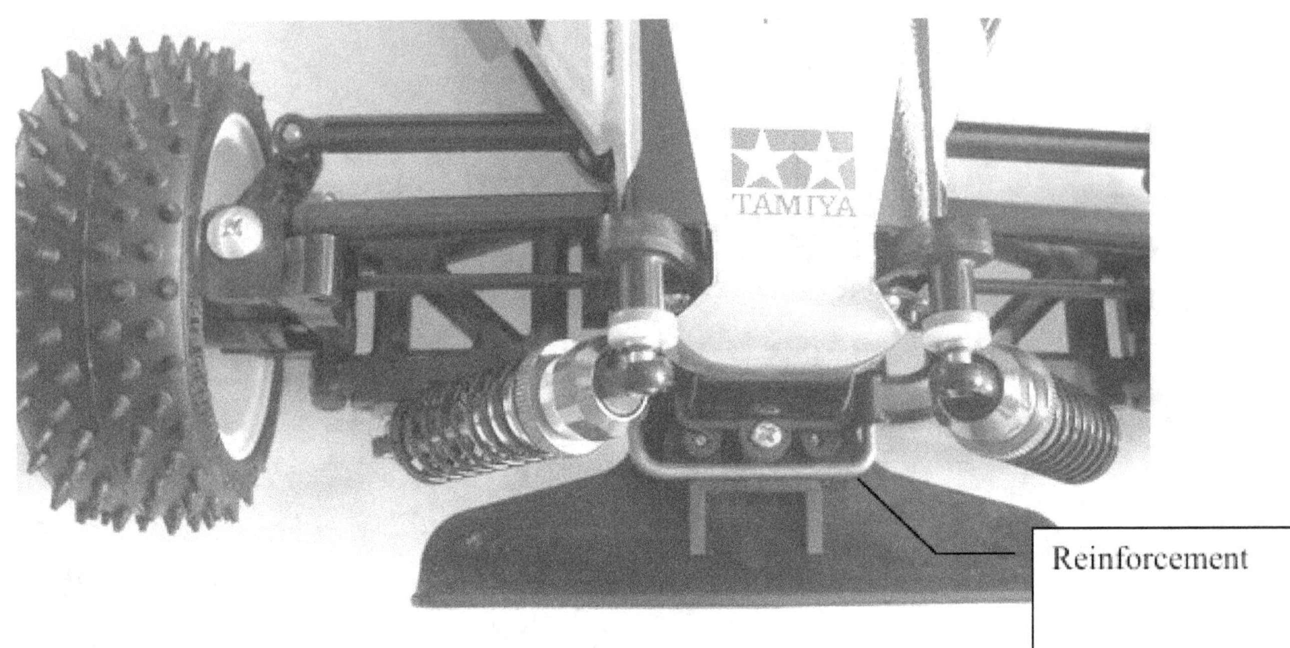

Reinforcement

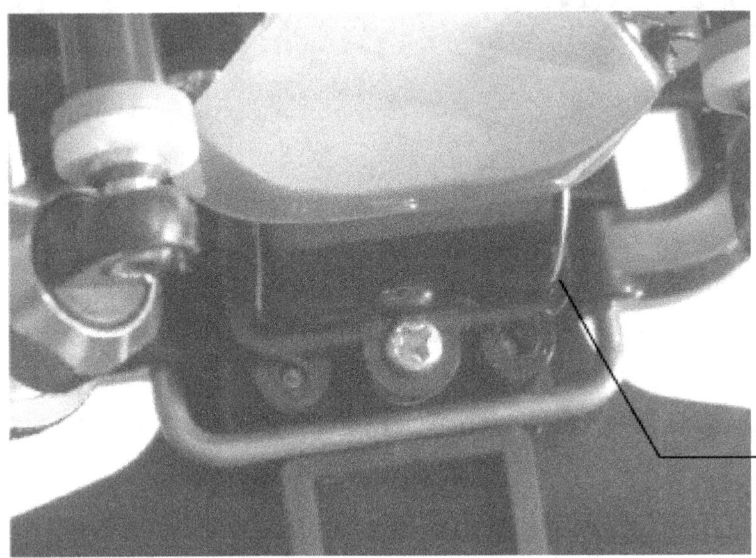

A closer look at the reinforcement mechanism

Always keep in mind, since the primary purpose of a bumper is impact absorption, plastic bumper is preferable over a full metal one (as it can offer better flexibility during a crash).

Another worry is on the side – when the buggy goes sideway, a sideway crash can occur. For beginners in particular it is important to have adequate protection on both sides of the chassis. This is why you should always have the lexan body shell on – it provides side and top protection in the case of crash or roll over.

Truck and truggy usually come with even stronger protection front and rear. They usually use larger bumpers on both ends.

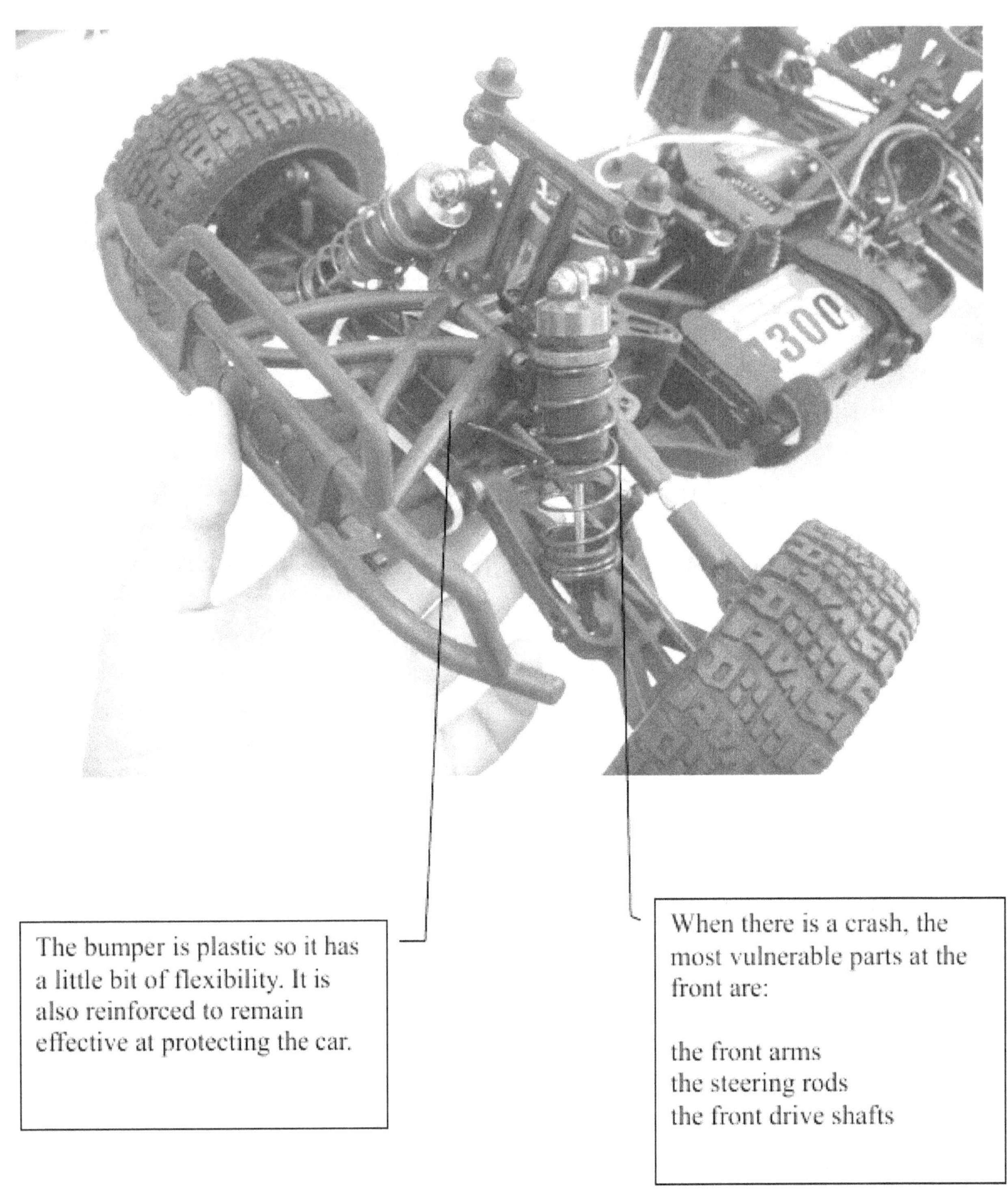

The bumper is plastic so it has a little bit of flexibility. It is also reinforced to remain effective at protecting the car.

When there is a crash, the most vulnerable parts at the front are:

the front arms
the steering rods
the front drive shafts

Reinforcement. There is a good reason
to use plastic here – you want the
bumper to adsorb the shock, not to pass
the shock to the body.

The lexan body shell provides side and top protection in the case of crash or roll over. It is therefore highly important that you drive the truck with the lexan body shell on it.

A short course truck is for jumping AND bashing. To protect against impact from bashing, there has to be protection around the car body. The tradeoff is weight. To sustain the weight, the power system must be able to deliver enough torque.

A typical brushless motor

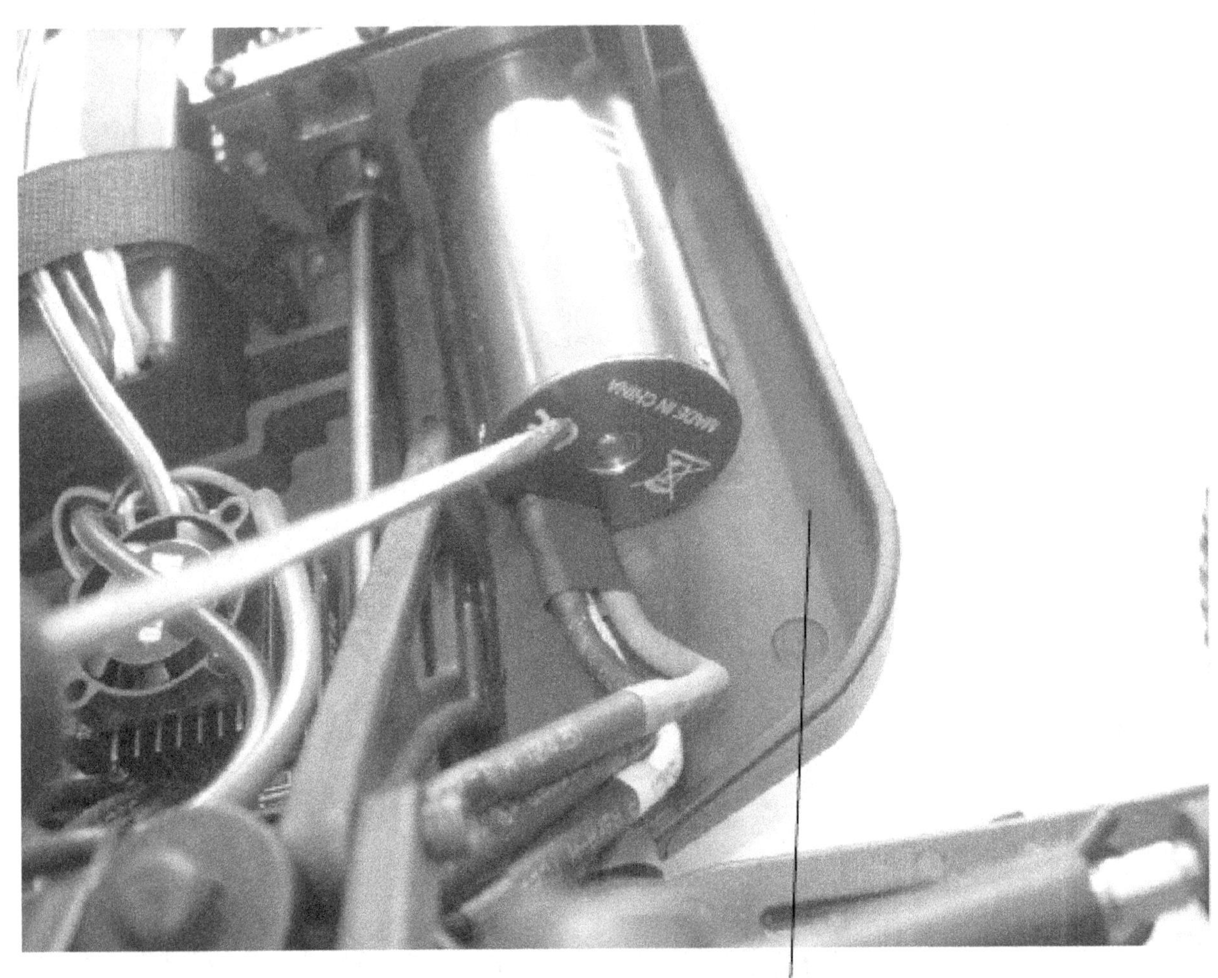

Short course trucks often run on muddy tracks. It is therefore appropriate to use a bath tube style body, to give the electronic components better protection against mud and rocks.

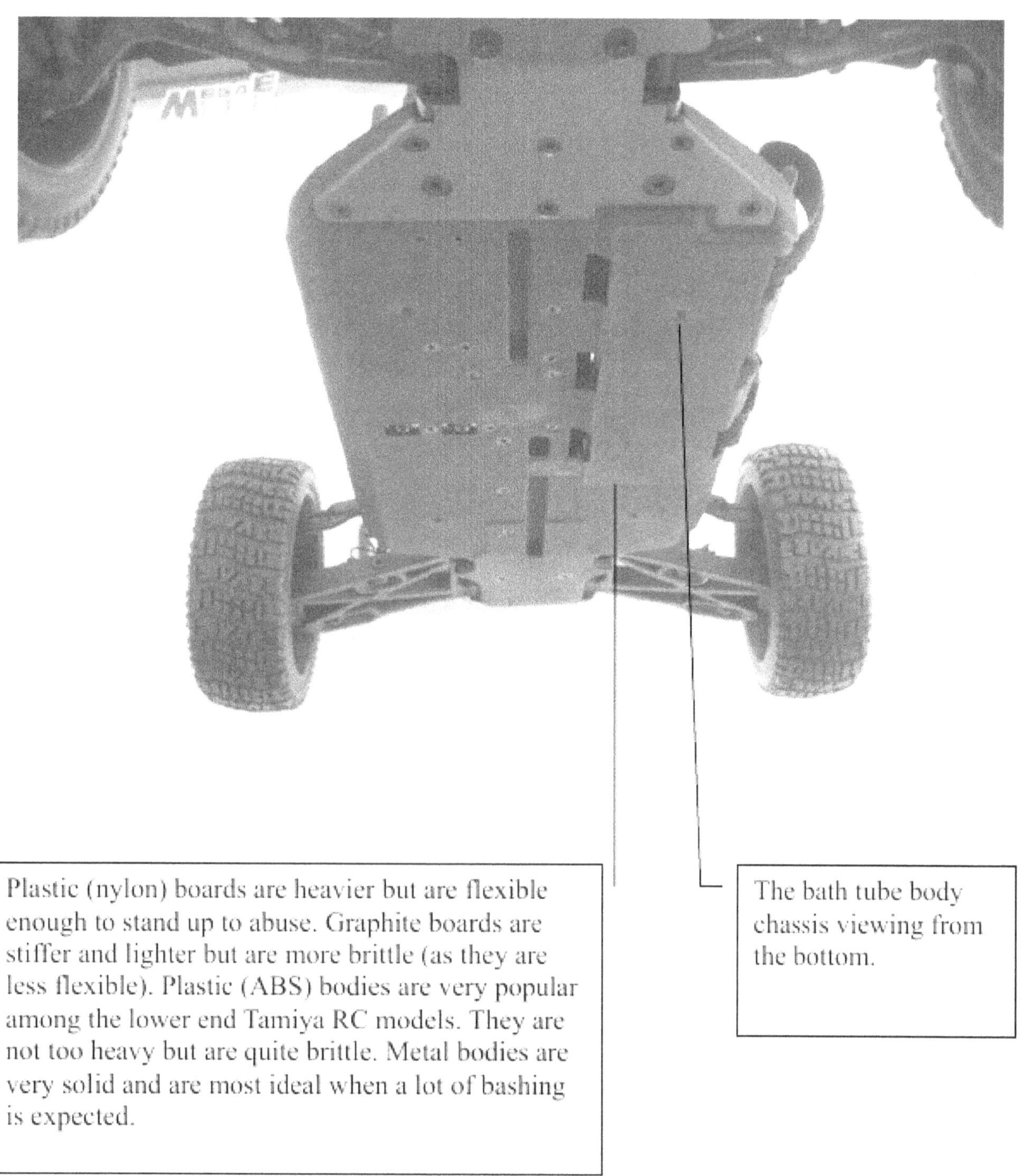

Plastic (nylon) boards are heavier but are flexible enough to stand up to abuse. Graphite boards are stiffer and lighter but are more brittle (as they are less flexible). Plastic (ABS) bodies are very popular among the lower end Tamiya RC models. They are not too heavy but are quite brittle. Metal bodies are very solid and are most ideal when a lot of bashing is expected.

The bath tube body chassis viewing from the bottom.

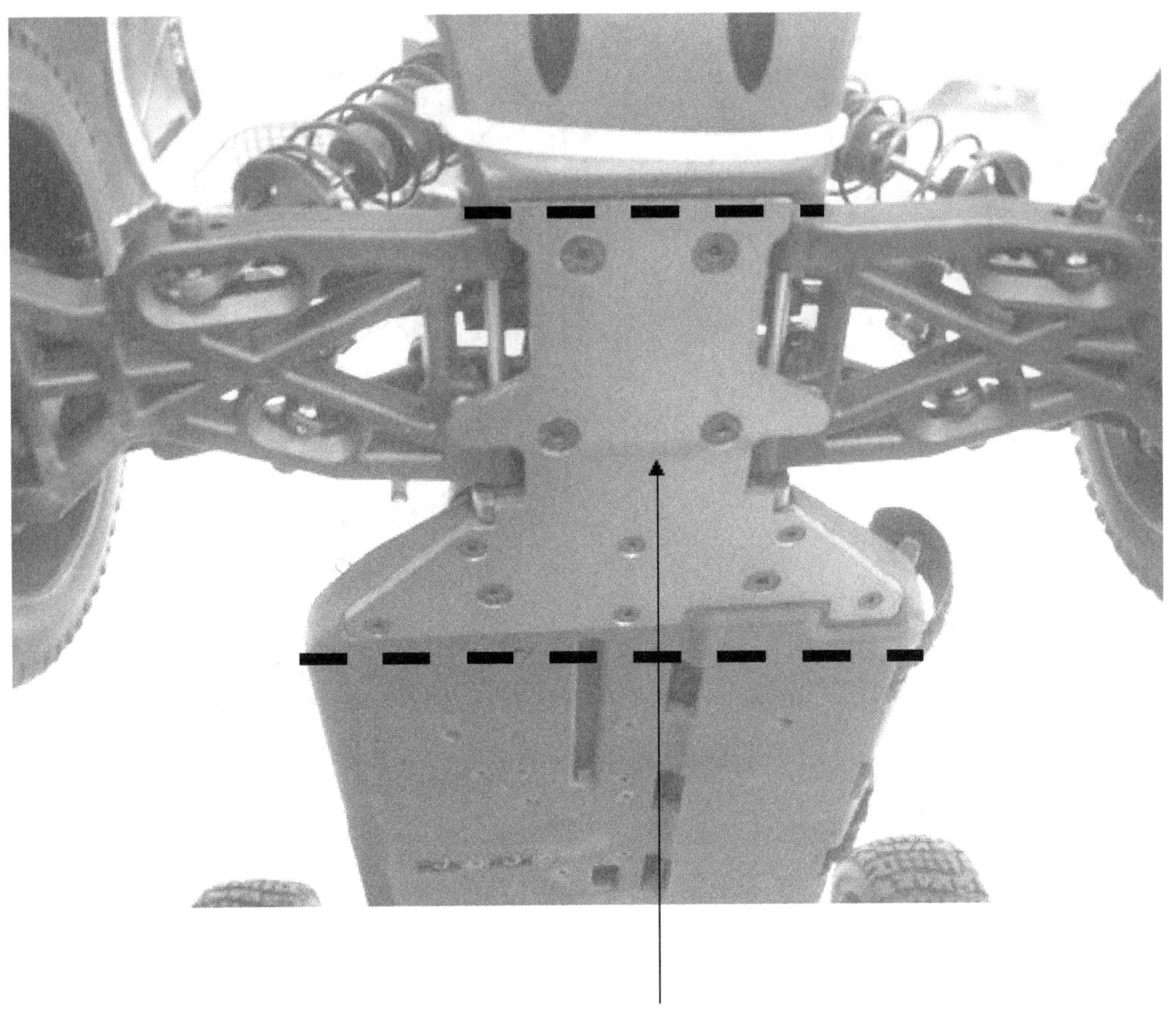

Metallic reinforcement is often deployed at the front section to improve structural strength. You will especially need it if the truck tends to land with the front after a jump.

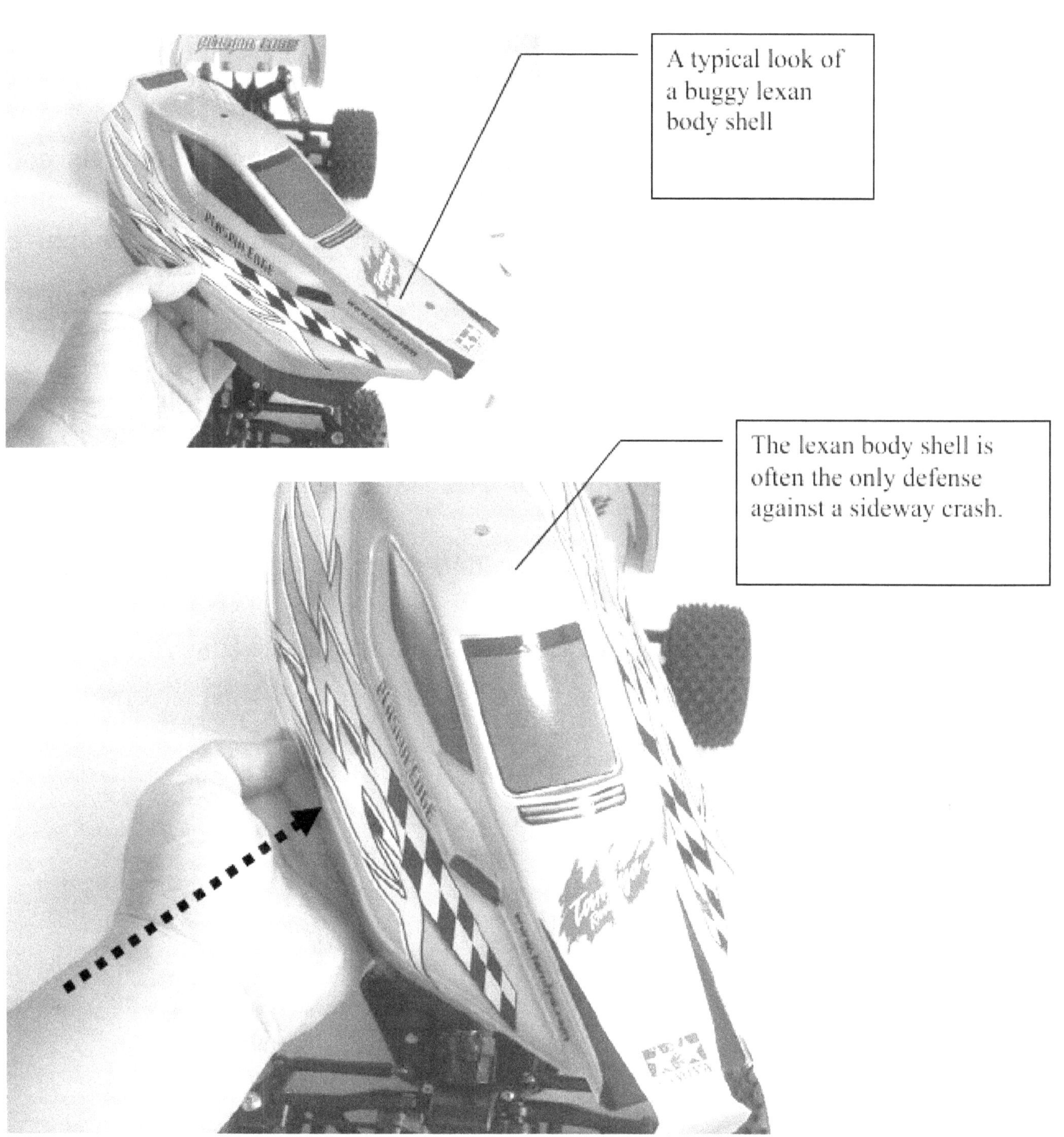

When you shop for a new RC buggy, one primary consideration is the chassis. Factors that deserve your attention include weight, sturdiness, and battery compartment. Plastic (nylon) boards are heavier but are flexible enough to stand up to abuse. Graphite boards are stiff and light but are highly expensive. Plastic (ABS) bodies are very popular among the lower end RC models. They are not too heavy but are quite brittle. Metal chassis is very strong and solid. However, it is heavier and more costly. Our demo buggy comes with a plastic ABS body out of the box. Tamiya is almost always ABS.

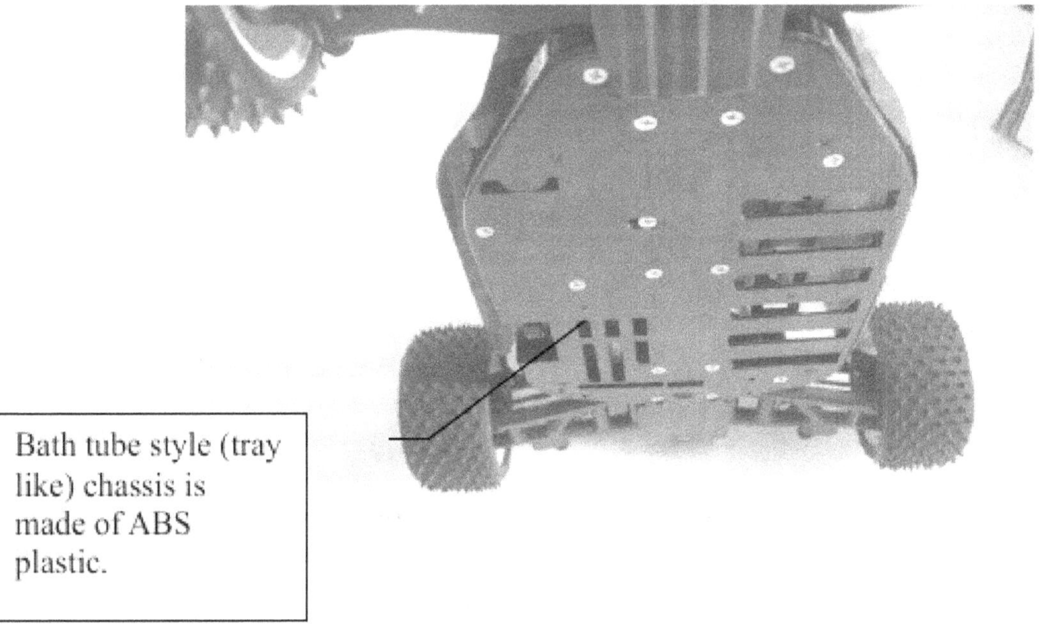

Bath tube style (tray like) chassis is made of ABS plastic.

Body structure reinforcement often involves the introduction of extra tailor-made parts (or the replacement of certain stock parts with something more heavy and solid), therefore weight increase (together with poorer energy efficiency and loss of speed) is hardly avoidable. The ideal choice of reinforcement material (if you are going to tailor make reinforcement parts) is graphite. It is strong, light and easy to cut. However, it is relatively expensive and may not be readily available (3Racing does have graphite reinforcement parts for certain Tamiya models). Metal is rock solid but is heavy.

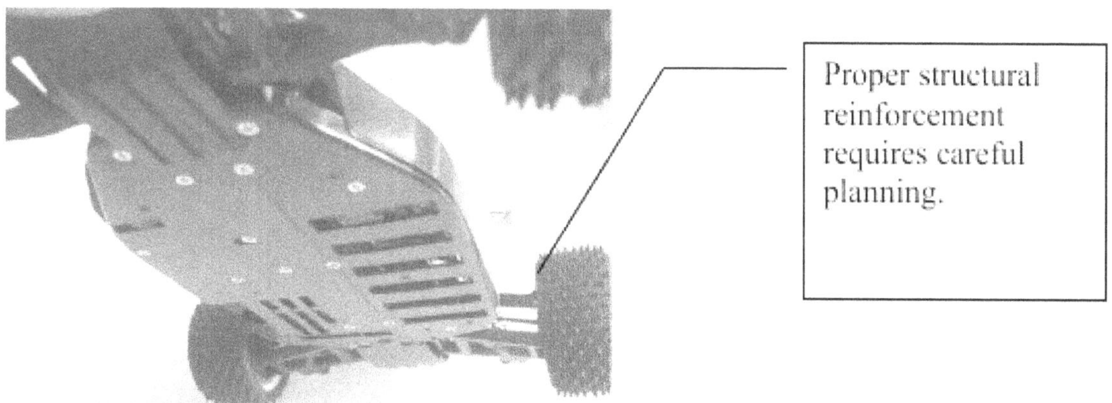

Proper structural reinforcement requires careful planning.

OVERVIEW OF THE 4WD ARCHITECTURE

The demo unit is a 4WD. Offroad car does not have to be 4WD

although 4WD is way more popular.

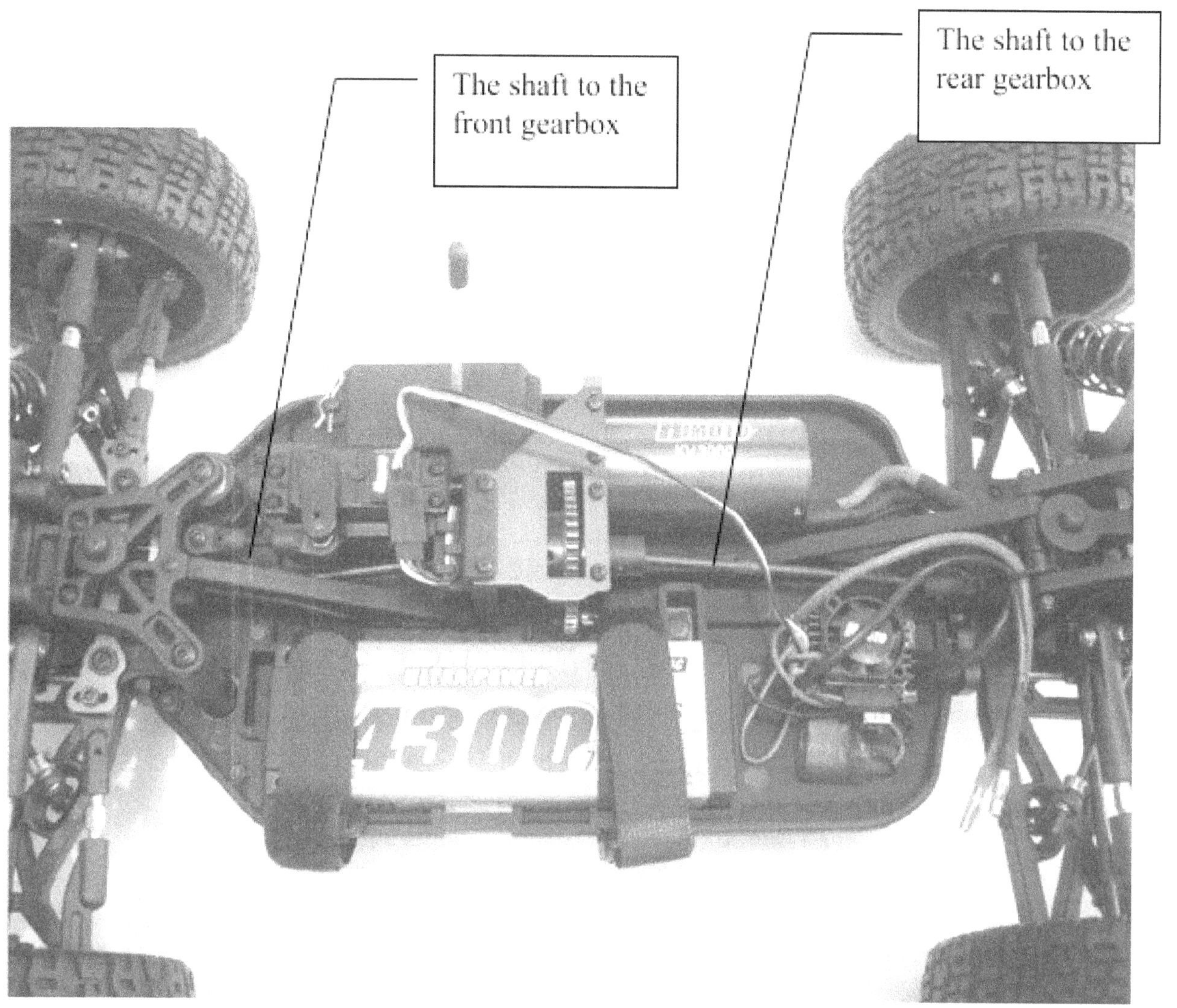

The reason? In 2WD (FWD and RWD), the traction of only two wheels is used (the other two are just rolling along). When more torque is applied than there is traction available (you accelerate too sudden and too much), the two powered wheels will break lose and start spinning. When the tires are spinning, your car may start to lose traction (and you may start to lose control). It is believed that RWD is even worse than FWD in this regard.

If your car needs more torque to accelerate (you need more torque for acceleration. Once you accelerated to a desired speed level, you need more rpm to maintain that speed), more accompanying traction must be available in order to avoid slipping wheels and maintain control over the car. In 2WD, the entire driving force is directed towards only two tires. In 4WD, the driving force is "shared" among four tires. Since each tire in a 4WD setting has to support a much smaller torque load, the tires are less likely to break lose.

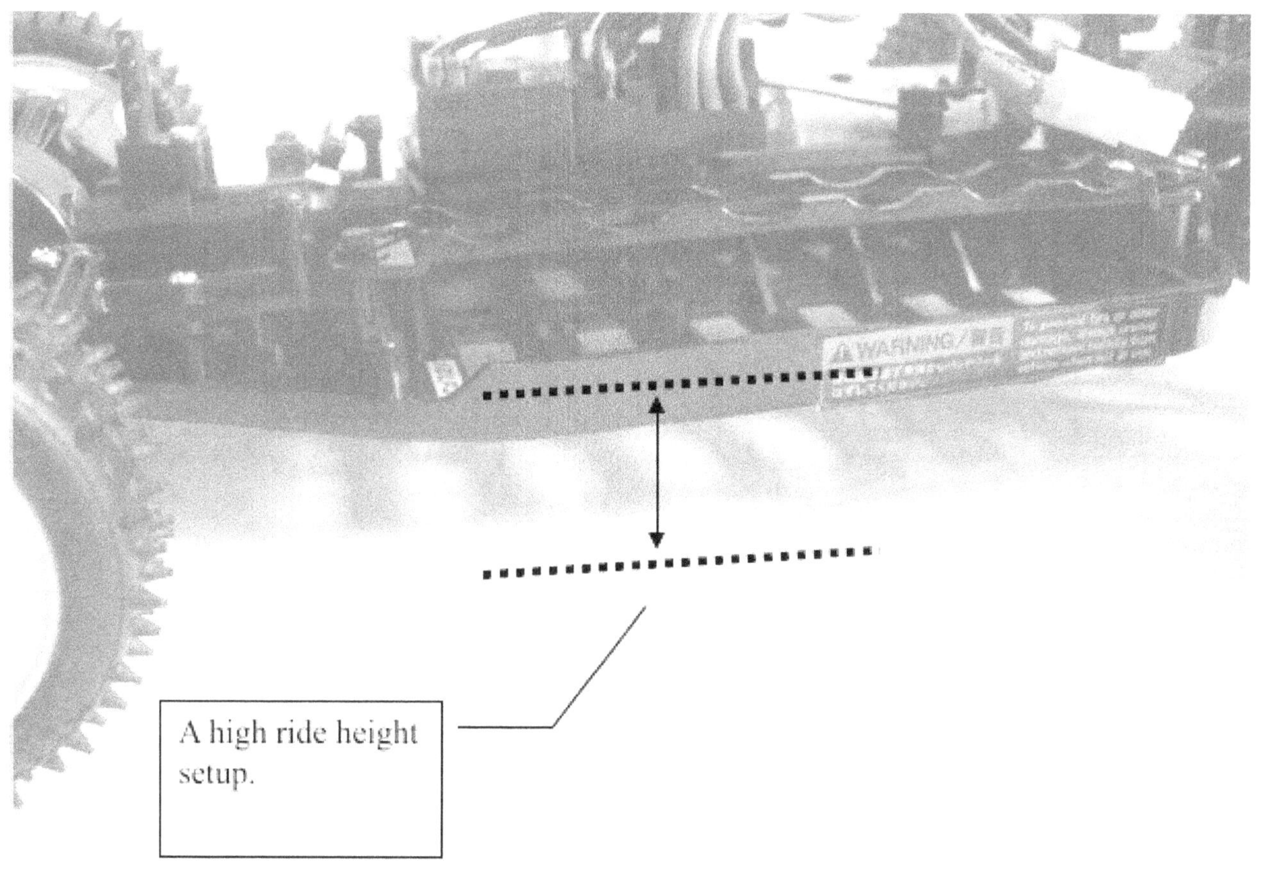

Offroad car jumps a lot. It therefore needs a high ride height. A low ride height tends to give better stability. It can be achieved by using shorter suspension arms and shorter oil dampers. HOWEVER, it can lead to easy chassis breakage during or after jumps.

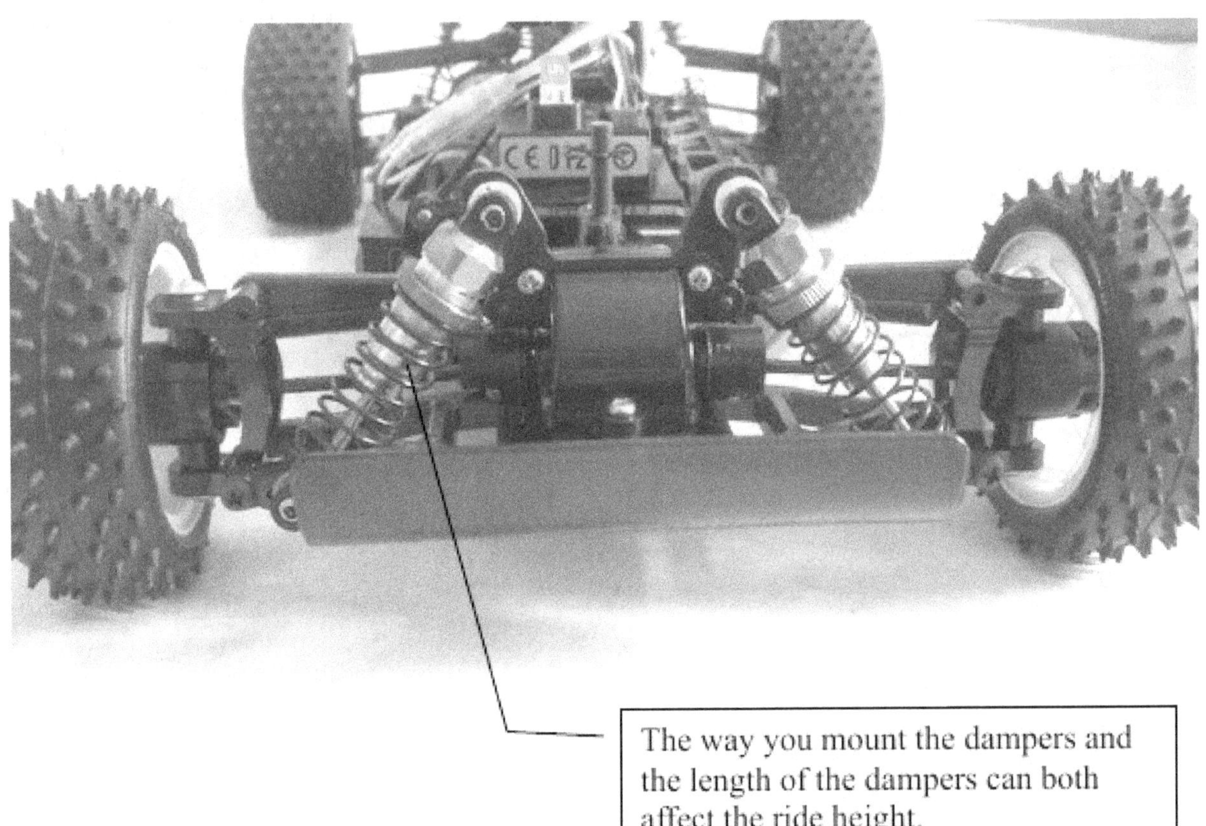

Truck and truggy tend to have high ride height. A high ride

height can be achieved by using long suspension arms and long oil

dampers.

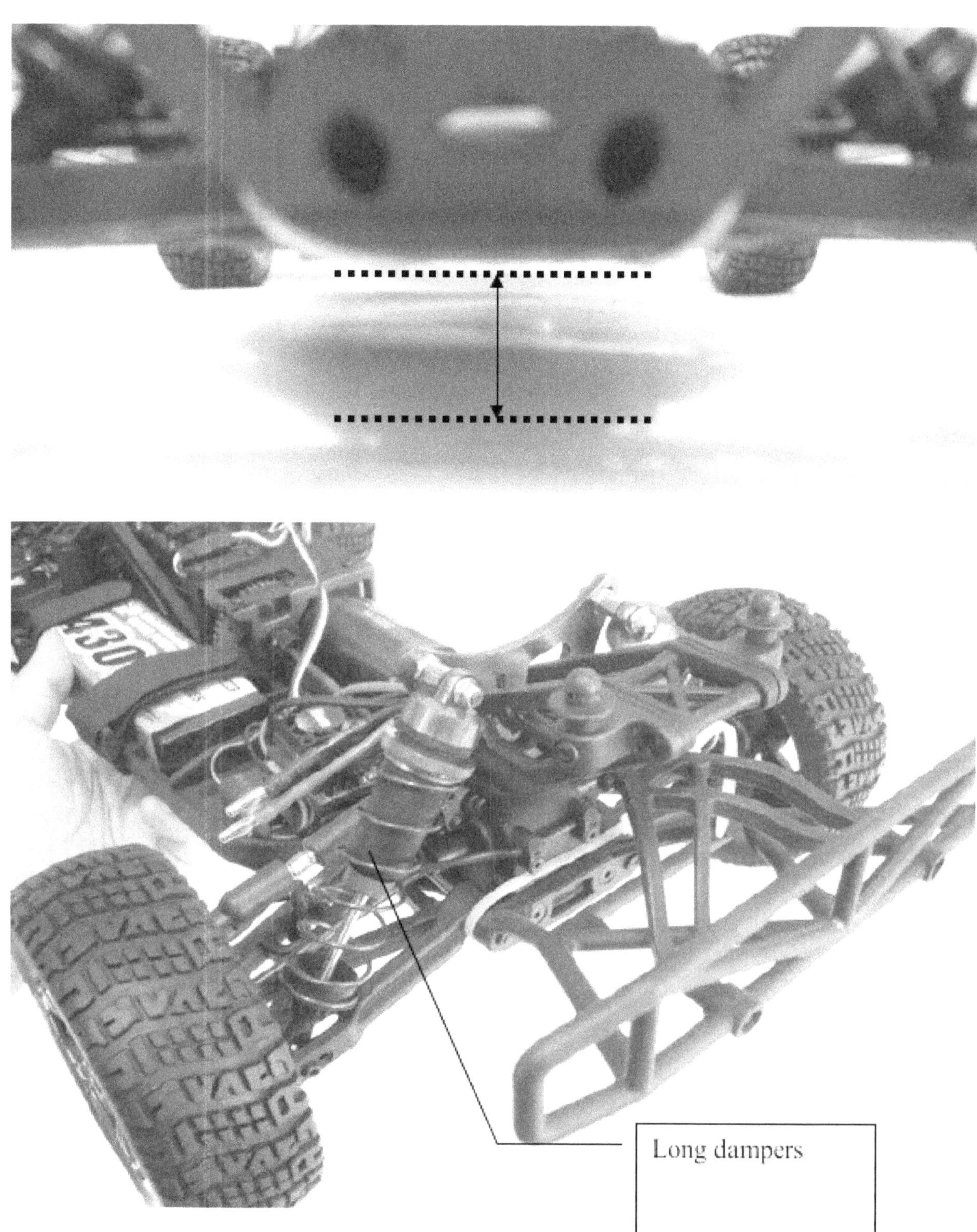

Long dampers

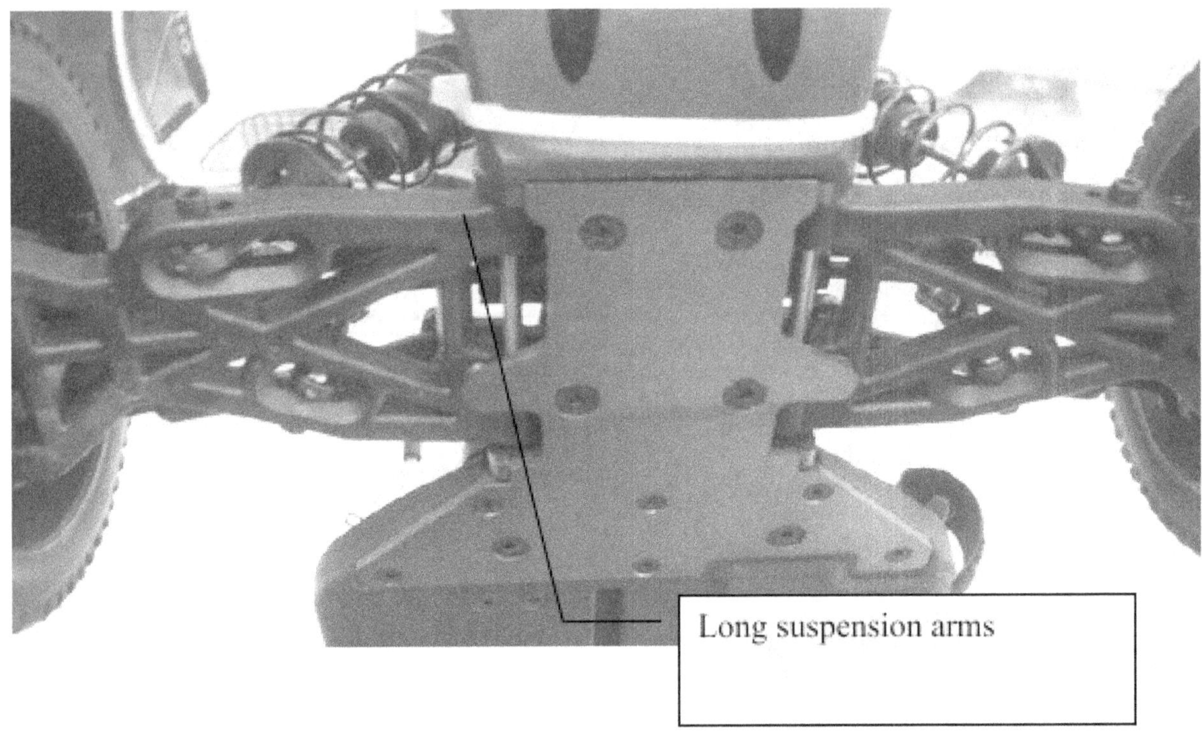

Due to the fact that most offroad cars have their motor placed closer to the backend of the chassis, the rear and front ride heights tend to be uneven (the heavier side goes lower).

An artificially configured "lower front" can benefit steering but is easier to go "diving" (which can make the buggy slides) when you brake real hard. The thing is, there isn't much you can do to redistribute the body weight through rearranging the component locations. Therefore, should imbalance of weight be undesirable, all you can do is to adjust the front and rear suspension systems accordingly.

Longer dampers are usually installed at the rear end.

The sturdiness of the chassis largely depends on the chassis layout. Our demo buggy has a bath tube chassis with reinforcement at the center, which is strong and flexible.

Reinforcement (also serves as shaft cover)

The main chassis board

OVERVIEW OF THE STRUCTURE AND THE MAJOR COMPONENTS

You can briefly divide the structure of an offroad car into 3 sections: the front, the middle and the rear.

The front section includes the steering mechanism and the front gearbox. The middle section includes the electronics, the battery and possibly the motor (if the motor is located at the middle of the chassis). The rear section includes the rear gearbox. Some buggies have the motor located at the rear end. Very few of them have their motor located at the front.

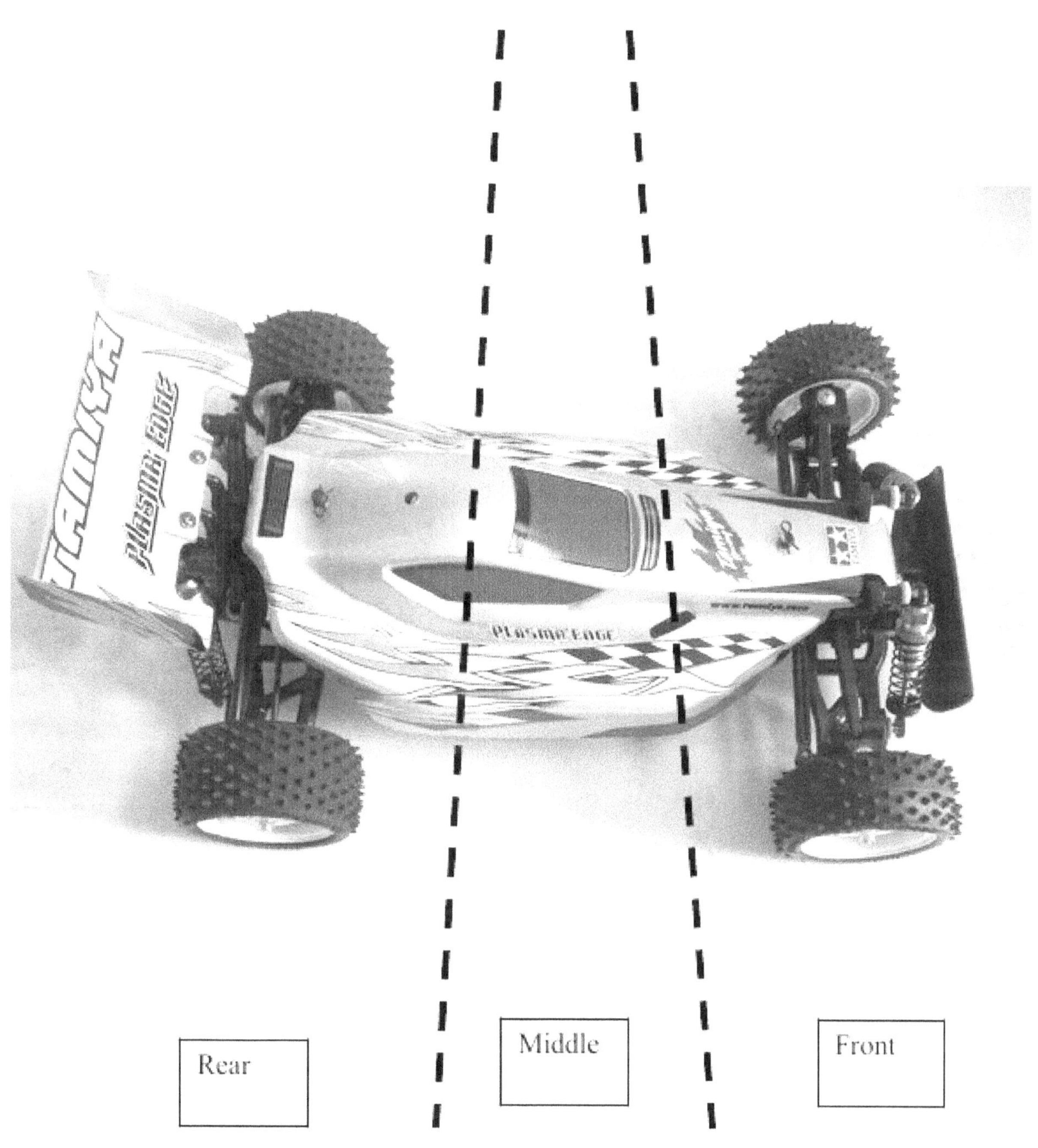

Rear
Middle
Front

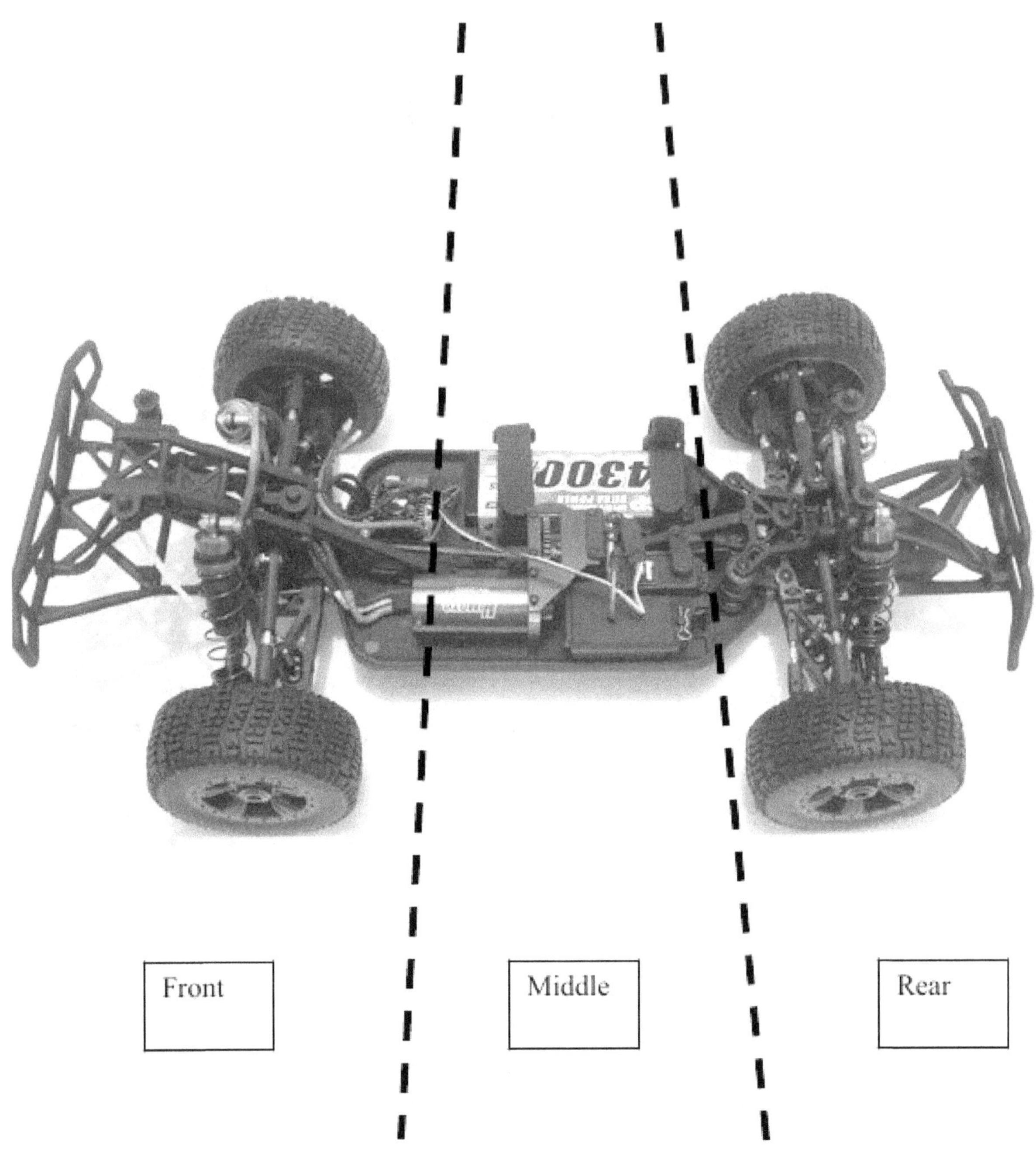

Front
Middle
Rear

UNDERSTANDING THE STEERING MECHANISM

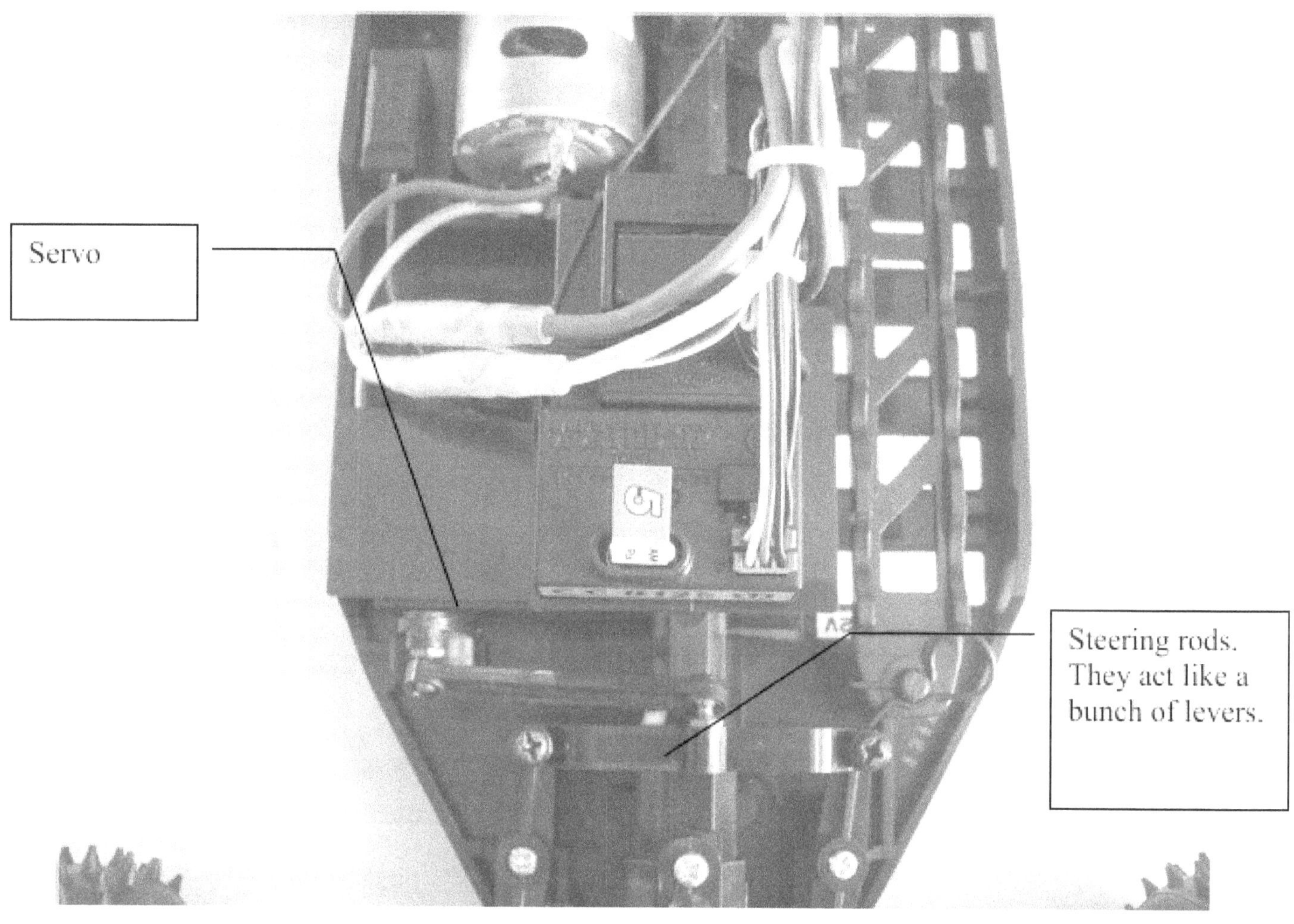

Servo saver
Servo

A servo (servomechanism) is a device for providing mechanical control remotely. RC servos use an electric motor for creating mechanical force and giving rotary output.

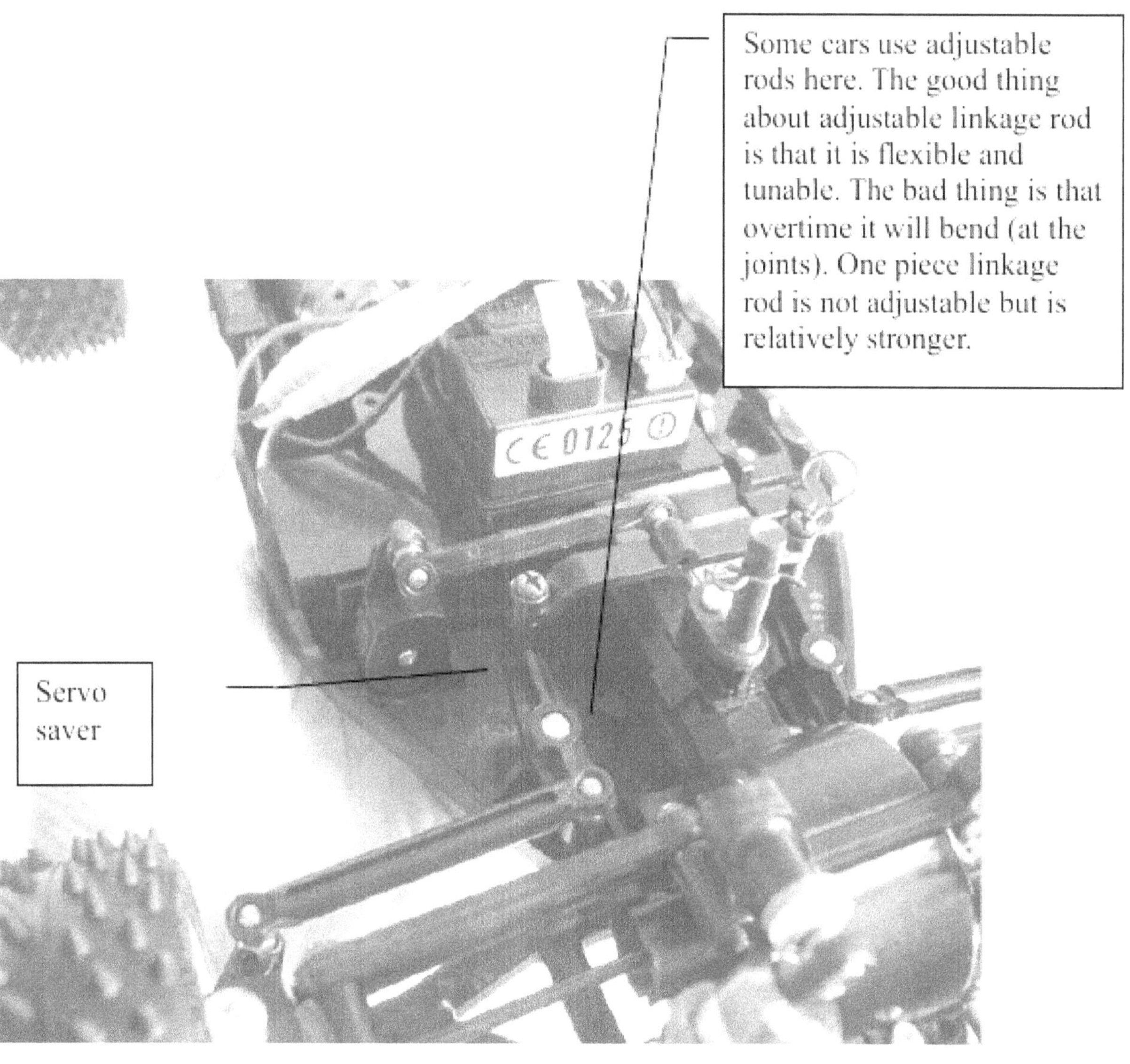

Modern RC cars rely on servo primarily for steering (in the past another servo was used for speed control when ESC was not the mainstream). Some servos have built-in metal gears so they are less likely to break. Honestly, for normal racing it is very unlikely that you can break the servo UNLESS you are doing something extremely crazy.

Coreless motor servo and cored motor servo share the same design concept, with totally different assemblies. The in-depth tech details are out of the scope of this book. Generally speaking, coreless motors are of lighter weight and are capable of responding/accelerating/decelerating faster and smoother, with better precision and more power. And of course, they are more expensive than their cored counterparts.

A servo saver is a piece of plastic device with a built-in spring for connecting the steering rods to the servo's output shaft. Its primary use is to absorb shock during driving or upon a crash. It is breakable, and in fact you want it to break upon a crash such that the servo itself can be free from any impact.

Without a proper saver, if the wheels get stuck during a turn it is possible to break the gears inside the servo.

The steering rods are all adjustable. They act like a bunch of levers.

The joint is ball-shaped (aka ball joint).

The good thing about adjustable
linkage rod is that it is flexible
and tunable. The bad thing is
that overtime it will bend (at the
joints).

UNDERSTANDING THE DRIVE SYSTEM, THE SHAFTS AND THE TIRES

The demo buggy shows a shaft drive system. The motor is placed at the middle, with a gear that drives a central drive shaft.

The motor drives the central shaft that connects the front and rear gearboxes.

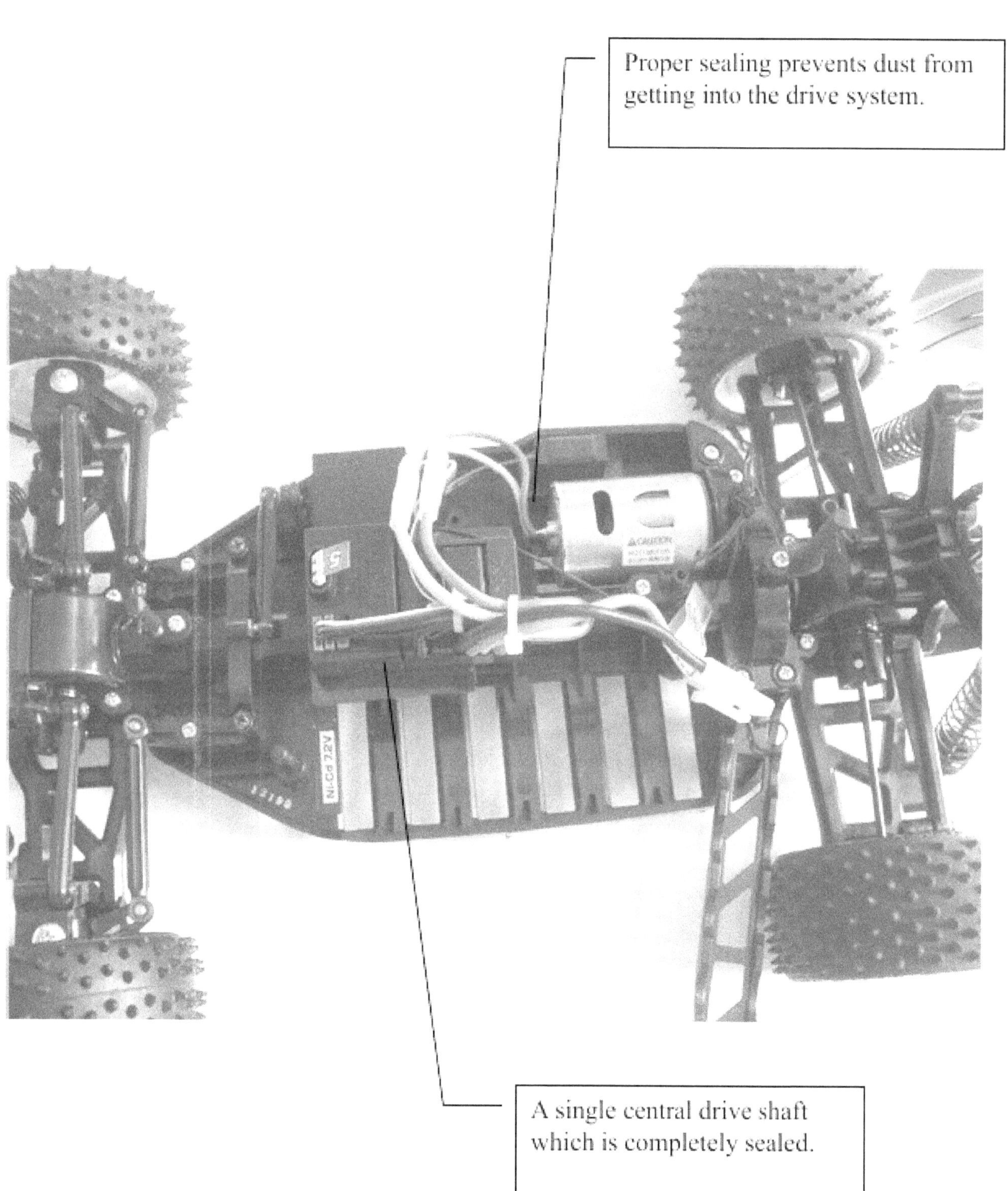

Proper sealing prevents dust from getting into the drive system.
A single central drive shaft which is completely sealed.

The motor should not be sealed. It needs proper air circulation to carry heat away.

Spur gear inside, which is attached to the central shaft.

Motor pinion inside, which is attached to the motor shaft.

Shaft drive gives better response and controllable power on demand. As long as the gearboxes are properly sealed, it is hassle free and almost maintenance free (it is much more difficult to break a shaft than a belt after all). Almost no tuning is required on the shaft. However, a shaft drive system is heavier (due to the use of more gears) and is usually much louder during acceleration. Also, if the chassis flexes then the gears may be bound by the shaft, which could lock up the tires and "jam" the buggy entirely.

The demo truck also has a shaft drive system. The motor is placed at the middle, with a gear that drives TWO separate shafts. In fact, very few modern trucks use a belt system. Some buggies do have retained the belt system (Kyosho Optima re-release, Schumacher Cat rerelease ...etc).

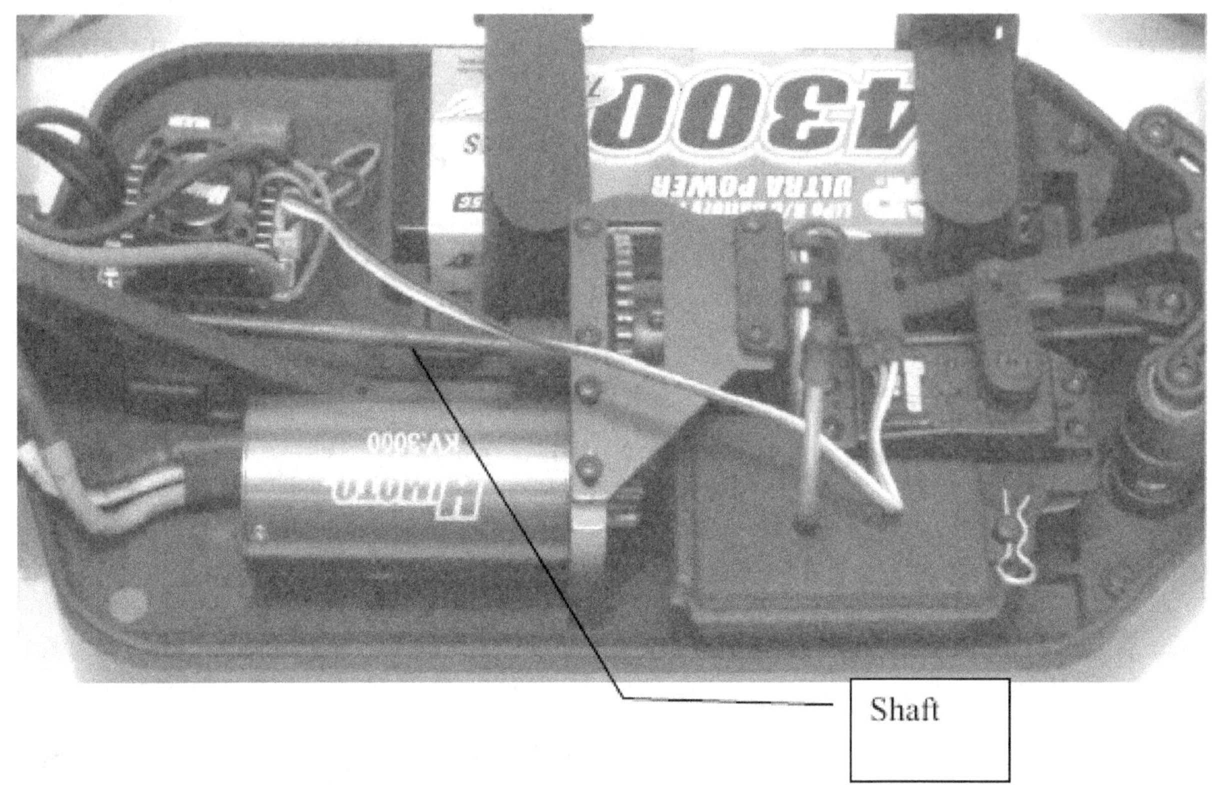

Shaft drive gives better response and controllable power on demand. As long as the drive system is properly sealed, it is hassle free and almost maintenance free (it is much more difficult to break a shaft than a belt after all). Almost no tuning is required on the shaft.

However, a shaft drive system is heavier (due to the use of more gears) and is usually much louder during acceleration. Also, if the chassis flexes then the gears may be bound by the shaft, which could lock up the tires and "jam" the car entirely. The demo car uses TWO separate shafts, which is a bit more flexible then using a single long shaft.

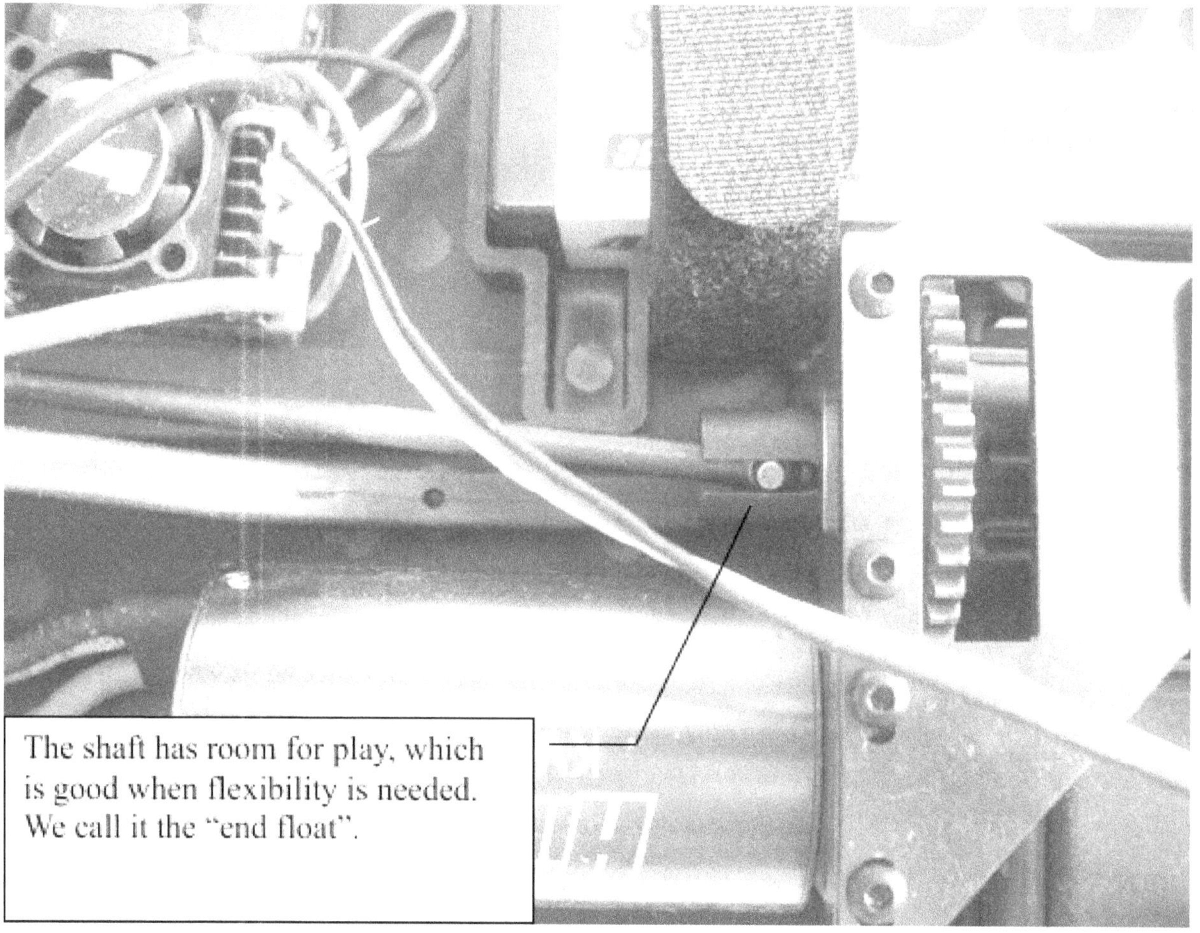

The shaft has room for play, which is good when flexibility is needed. We call it the "end float".

Belt drive has a simpler design due to the use of less gears along the drive chain, and it keeps the weight down for the same reason. It tends to run quieter as well. However, the belt is more subject to wear and tear (it will start weakening and stretching over time) especially upon frequent hard accelerations and you will need to regularly adjust its tension just to prevent it from skipping. Also, it is widely believed that belt drive car often induces drag (i.e. belt drag), which can make the drive system quite inefficient. An improperly sealed belt drive system is another source of problem – it can get stuck easily if dust and unknown debris find their way into it.

If you race in an area with extreme weather conditions, go for a shaft driven 4WD. The rubber material used by some belts is very sensitive to differing weather conditions (too cold VS too hot) and may require frequent tension re-adjustment.

Every wheel is driven through an independent dog bone shaft. There is a hub-like socket on each end of the shaft. The hub is "held" by a larger bushing or ball bearing.

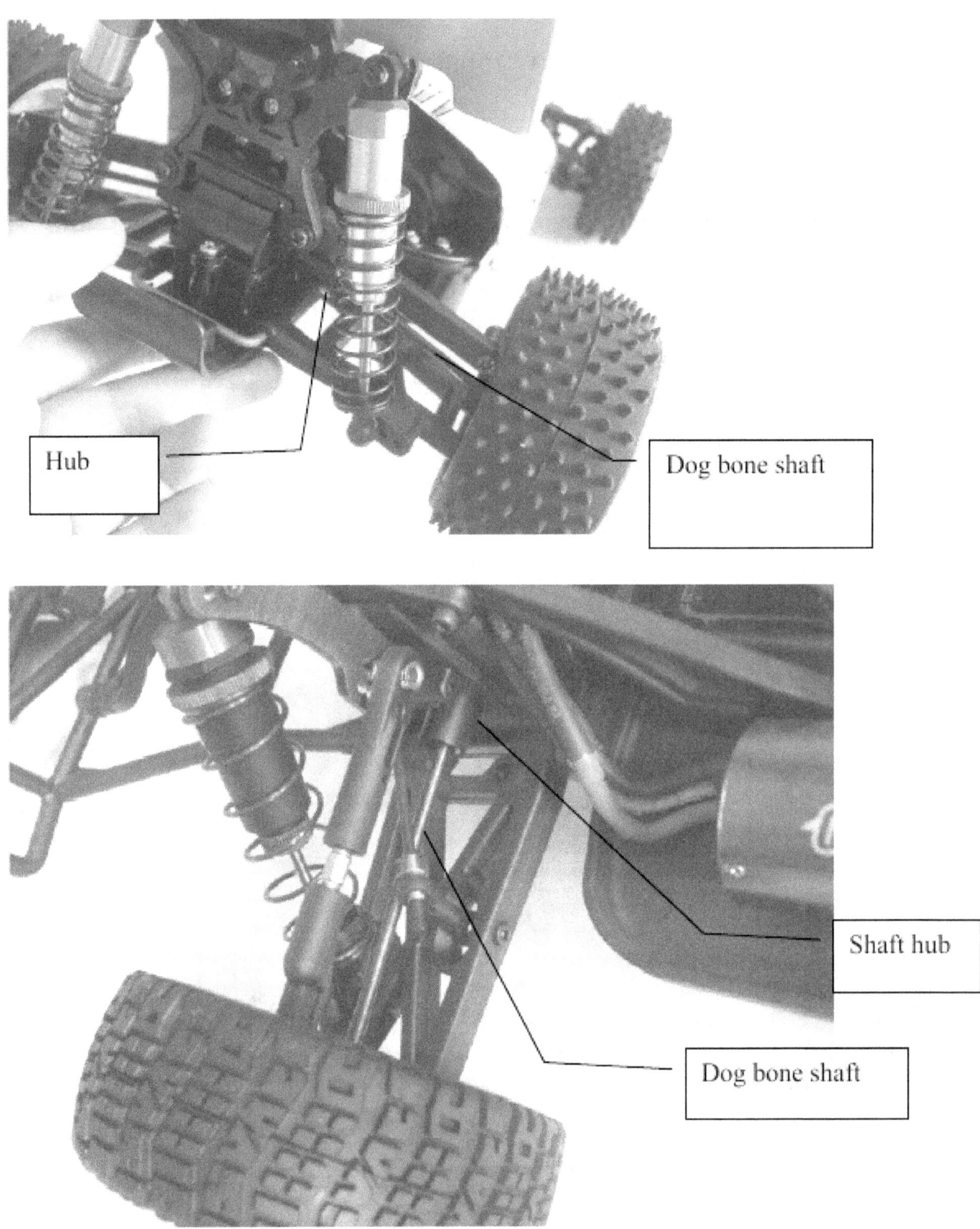

Hub
Dog bone shaft
Shaft hub
Dog bone shaft

If you adjust the stock suspension settings (damper, mounting point ...etc) you may need to check and ensure the dog bones are stilling doing good when spinning. At each end (or on at least one end) of the dog bone there has to be room for "float" and flexibility. However, too much room for float could introduce problem as well. You may find it necessary to add an end pad to each side (or to at least one side) of the dog bone. The end pad does not need to be thick, but it better be made of a flexible material, such as rubber (small rubber O ring will do the job). The goal is to allow for float while filling up the empty room for preventing meaningless "play" of the dog bone.

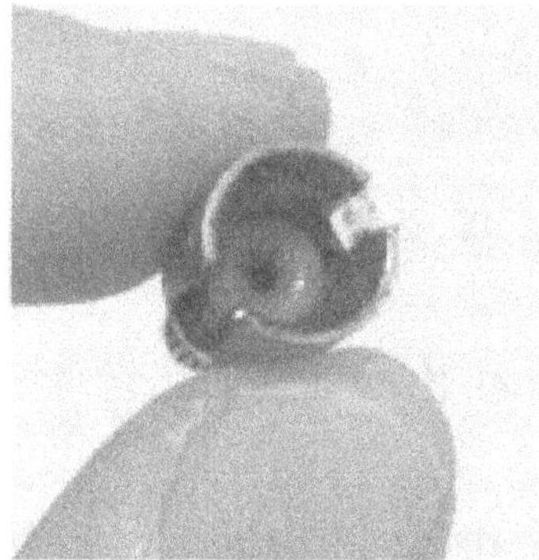

Also remember, there is a need to regularly clean bearings that are exposed to dust and dirt (such as those installed on the outer side of the gear case and those attached to the uprights). One quick and easy way to clean bearings is to flush them with silicon oil spray.

Tread tires have treads for channeling down any water or dust encountered on the track and can provide maximum grip out of the ground. There are hundreds of tread patterns available, although the actual pattern itself is mostly a mix of functionality and aesthetics. Pin tires are solely for off road racing where the tracks are bumpy and dusty (or wet) or that traction is totally absent. Buggies often deploy pin tires.

Some tread designs are unidirectional, meaning the tire has a desired rotation direction for enhancing straight-line acceleration through reducing rolling resistance. It is therefore important for you not to put a 'clockwise' tire on the left hand side or a 'counter-clockwise' tire on the right side (check the tire's manual – it should tell you the correct installation direction).

Symmetrical tire, on the other hand, has a tread pattern consistent across the tire surface (meaning both halves of the tread face are of the same design) and is therefore not direction sensitive installation-wise. Buggy pin tires are usually NOT directional.

UNDERSTANDING THE BRUSHED MOTOR AND THE ESC

A brushed motor has 2 wires – RED and BLACK. Brushless motor

has an additional yellow wire.

Brushed motor has only two wires.

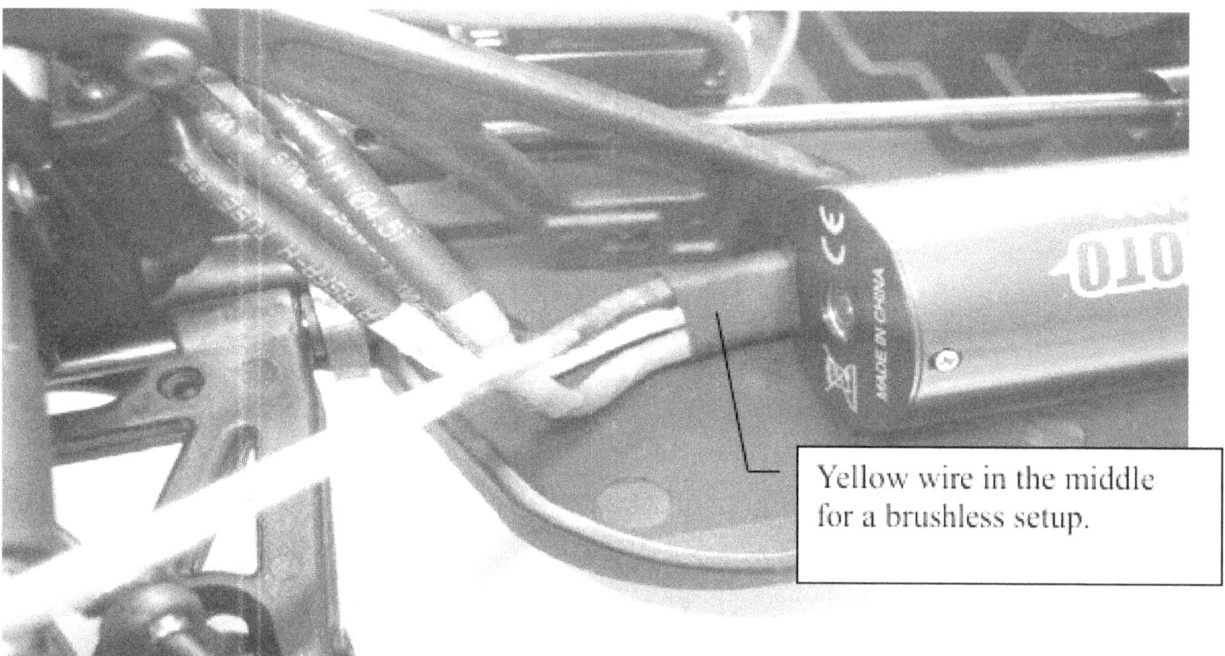

Yellow wire in the middle for a brushless setup.

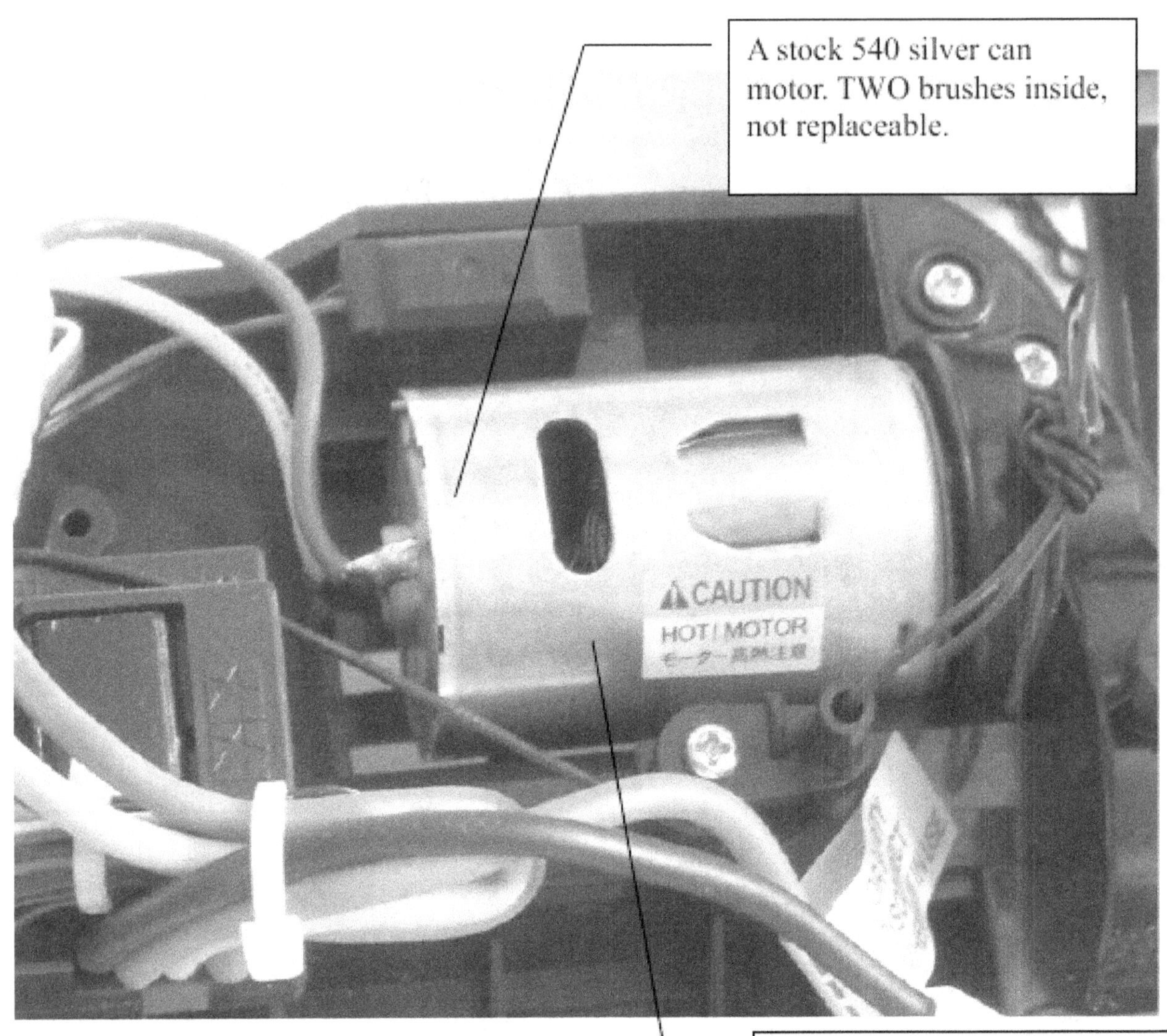

Do note that some Japanese manufacturers use GREEN and YELLOW wires in place of the traditional RED and BLACK wires.

The wires on the ESC side are light blue and orange. The idea is to avoid confusion with the battery connection.

Most off-the-shelf 1:10 RC kits are shipped with the RS540 motor. Most competition grade motors in the market are designed for substituting the RS540. When looking at their specifications, keep in mind that the "No Load" data is of relatively less importance because in the practical world there is always a load. What you care is how the motor performs under expected load.

There is a misconception that a standard 540 power is not powerful enough to be hot. This is not true. Modern Lipo power is pushing the limit and a 540 can and will get very hot especially when Summer is approaching!

People always wonder if a 550 will work on a standard RC car. In this video we have a Tamiya Hotshot equipped with a 7.4V 550 strong magnet motor. It is longer than a 540 but cars such as the Hotshot (which mount the motor sideway) usually have enough room for it since there is nothing on the side that contains or covers the end cap. This motor gives much better torque without losing its top speed. It also produces way less heat than a 540. In my opinion it is a very good choice for offroad use.

The 560 is even longer. It produces even higher torque. However, it requires higher voltage as well for delivering higher rpm. It runs optimally at 18V. If you give it 7.4V it will run quite slow. It has a shorter shaft so it may not work for some configurations where the pinion has to be installed in reverse direction.

Motor turns describe the number of times the wires are wrapped around the armature web of the motor. The less turns a motor has, the faster it will go, and vice versa (so a 13T motor will run way faster than a 20T motor).

Motors with very few turns can consume battery power quickly and can also generate massive heat, therefore both your ESC and your battery (and the wires they use) must be strong enough to sustain the heavy load. In fact most modern ESCs are marketed with a rating specifying the "minimum number of turns" that can be sustained.

A lower turn motor such as a 15-T can produce greater RPM but slightly less torque than a higher turn motor. The drawback - running on a low turn motor will require frequent motor maintenance, such as cleaning and brushes replacement. The life span of such motor is generally short as they are way too easy to get overheated.

The general guideline is to pick a ESC with a capacity greater than that of the motor currently in use.

Capacity is measured in AMPS. The ESC has to be capable of handling the amp draw of the motor. If the motor needs to draw 35A, the ESC must be 35A or higher. A higher rating can provide a safety margin (higher rating ESCs can run cooler as well).

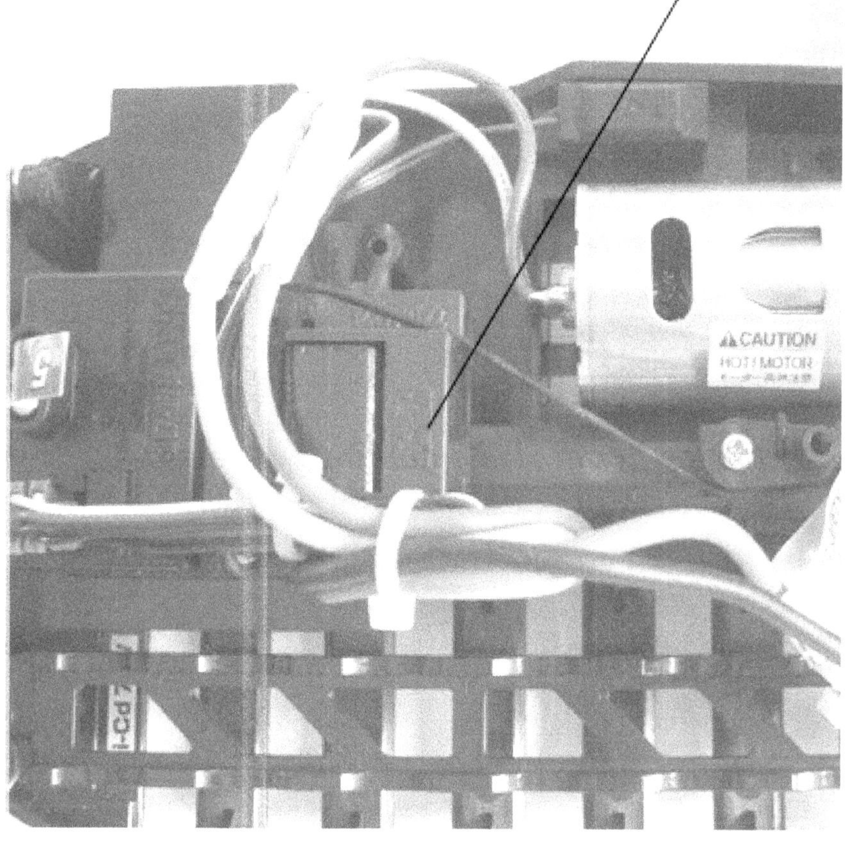

Motor current draw has many real world factors that need to be considered, including but not limited to vehicle weight, gearing, race track condition, drive style, battery voltage …etc. A fairly simple way is to run it with a fully charged battery. Re-charge the battery when done and see how much mAh is put back in by the charger (you need a computerized charger for it). Then you can calculate by hand the average current draw based on that mAh and the time ran.

The ESC is responsible for controlling speed, throttle and breaking. It also takes power from the battery on behalf of the motor, the receiver and the servo. In fact, all modern ESCs have battery eliminator circuit (BEC) built in for regulating voltage (5V) for the receiver so that the need for extra batteries can be eliminated.

A typical brushed ESC has 3 sets of connections: connection to the battery (2 wires); connection to the brushed motor (2 wires); and connection to the receiver (3 very thin wires).

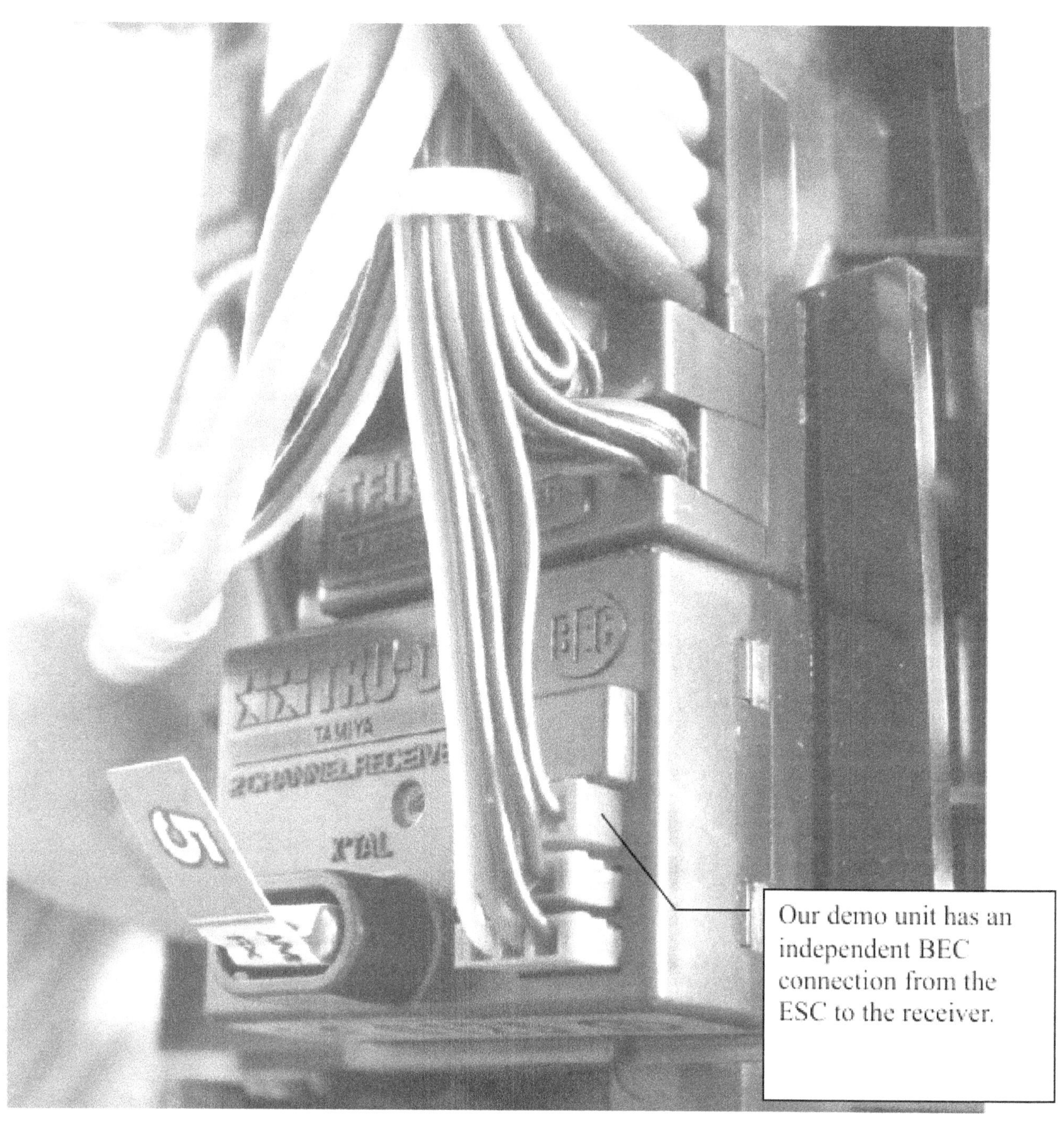

Our demo unit has an
independent BEC
connection from the
ESC to the receiver.

Heat is the primary source of harm for ESC. An ESC can get hot quickly if the motor is over geared or if the driveline is bound up. With the help of a heatsink the risk of overheating an ESC can be minimized. Seriously, you NEED the help of a heatsink almost all the time. Keep in mind, you need a heatsink that will physically match your ESC. **And always allow for sufficient air inflow to your ESC. Don't shield it unless straightly necessary. If air inflow is not sufficient, add a cooling fan.**

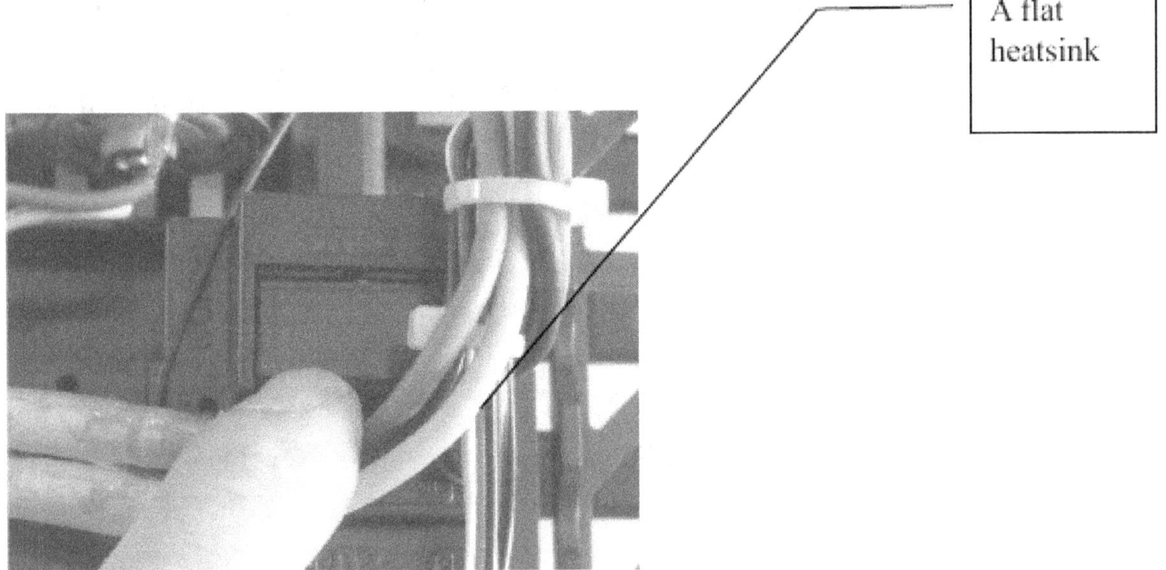

Using an over powered motor can cook your ESC almost

immediately. Using an over powered battery can achieve the same. If there is significant binding in the drive train somewhere along the line or if you are running under heavy sunshine, you can still cook up your ESC in a minute or two. Another alternative – use an upgrade friendly motor such as the Team Powers 540 black motor, which is faster than the stock motor and at the same time very ESC friendly. It is not as power hungry as other modified motors so ESC replacement is not necessary.

Traditional MSC can hardly be found now. It requires another servo to operate and is not reliable. The Tamiya Big Wing below

uses such MSC.

BRUSHLESS MOTOR AND ESC

A brushless motor uses an electronically-controlled commutation system instead of the traditional brush based commutation system. In a conventional brushed motor, the brushes make mechanical contact with a set of electrical contacts on the commutator for forming an electrical circuit between the DC electrical source and the armature coil-windings.

In a brushless motor, the brush-system/commutator assembly is replaced by an intelligent electronic controller which contains a bank of MOSFET devices to drive high-current DC power and a microcontroller to precisely orchestrate the rapid-changing current-timings.

There is a KV rating on every brushless motor. Our demo unit has a stock KV 3000 motor. Generally speaking, higher rating means the potential to be more powerful. A KV number means the number of RPM that can be provided by each volt of power. RPM is a measure of how fast the motor is rotating. So, for example, by powering a KV3000 motor with a 7.4V battery, this RPM can in theory be achieved: 3000 x 7.4 = 22200 rpm

The reason why we say this is theoretical is that the rating is under the assumption of "no load". In the world of brushless motor, it is said that Torque, Voltage, and RPM are all linearly related. That is, the amount of torque or RPM produced by the motor divided by the voltage input is more or less constant all the time. Still, in the real world, the motor is always under heavy load and there are many other factors that can come into play (such as manufacturing quality). In fact, when the motor is TOO fast the motor shaft may shatter from the speed...

The KV rating can give a GENERAL INDICATION to performance only. Torque is another important factor. Higher RPM usually means less torque. For a heavier truck you may need more torque than speed. Some people prefer to measure and indicate brushless motor power using the traditional turn system. A 4.5T motor is faster and with less torque when being compared to a

13.5T motor. Do keep in mind, a 13.5T brushless motor can be way more powerful than a 13T brushed motor!

Brushless motors offer higher reliability, longer lifetime (due to the absence of brush erosion and sparks), and overall reduction of electromagnetic interference. However, they are expensive to manufacture due to the need for high power MOSFET devices in the fabrication of its speed controller and the use of manual labor for winding the stator coils.

Brushless motors require the use of special purpose ESC. These special ESCs has 3 wires for connecting to the brushless motor. The general guideline is to pick a ESC with a capacity greater than that of the motor currently in use.

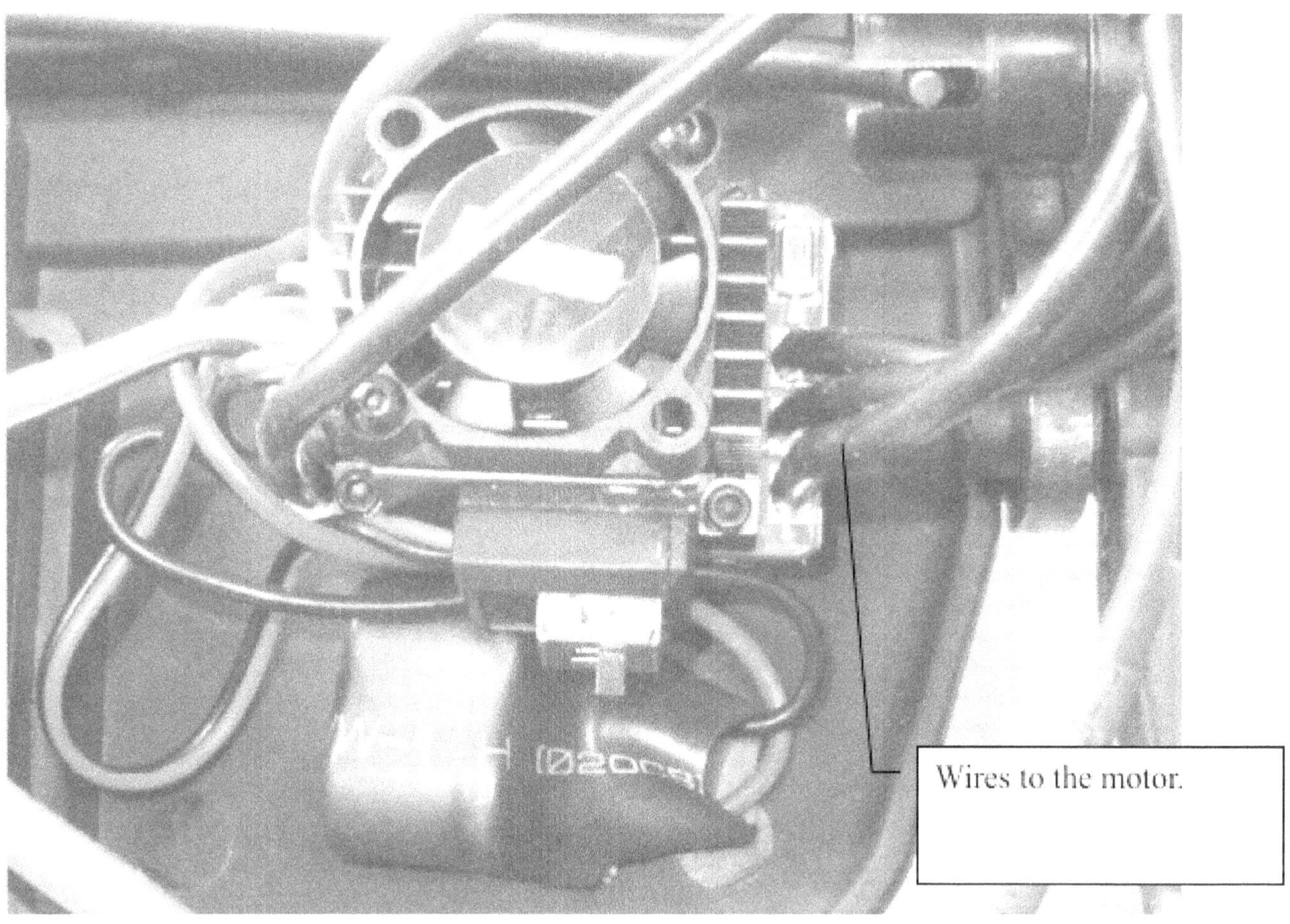

The yellow wire is for electronic control and feedback. It must be correctly connected. If the red/black wires are mismatched, the motor will spin in the opposite direction.

UNDERSTANDING BATTERY CONFIGURATION

Nowadays Lipo is the way to go. If the motor needs to draw in 35A, then your Lipo pack must be able to handle this as well. The rating can be found on the battery pack.

You want to know that lipo cells are rated at 3.7 volts per cell. For RC these are the most popular configurations:

3.7 V battery = 1 cell x 3.7 volts (1S)

7.4 V battery = 2 cells x 3.7 volts (2S)

11.1 V battery = 3 cells x 3.7 volts (3S)

14.8 V battery = 4 cells x 3.7 volts (4S)

For standard 1:10 buggies, truggies and trucks you need nothing over 7.4V. Some 1:8 heavy duty cars use 11.1V.

Lipo battery capacity is measured in milliamp hours (mAh). It tells how much drain can be put on the battery for an hour at which time the battery will be emptied out. Say if a battery is rated at 1000 mAh (that is, 1A), then it would be completely discharged in an hour with a 1A load imposed on it. If a motor needs to draw in 35A, the battery will be drained in several minutes.

The C rating is all about discharge rate. It tells how fast a battery can be discharged without introducing damage to the battery itself. If you have a very power-hungry motor, you will for sure need a battery with higher MAH and C values.

Voltage is less flexible. Most (but not all) ESCs for cars cannot support anything over 7.4V. You need to pick a battery that is safe for the ESC.

There are three connections on a Lipo pack. The + / - connections must not be mixed up or the ESC will get burnt instantly (unless the ESC comes with reverse polarity protection). The middle smaller connection is for balanced charging and is not for connecting to the ESC.

The battery-to-ESC
connections must
perfectly match – you
cannot reverse the + wire
and the - wire.

We call these banana plugs.

LiFE is a safer alternative to Lipo. It is safer in that it seldom explodes or burns when over-drawn. However, it is way less popular in the market. Also, it offers only 3.3V per cell, which is less "powerful" than the Lipo counterpart.

It is very important for you to check and ensure that the chassis has sufficient space for the Lipo pack. Some lipo packs are made slightly larger in size...

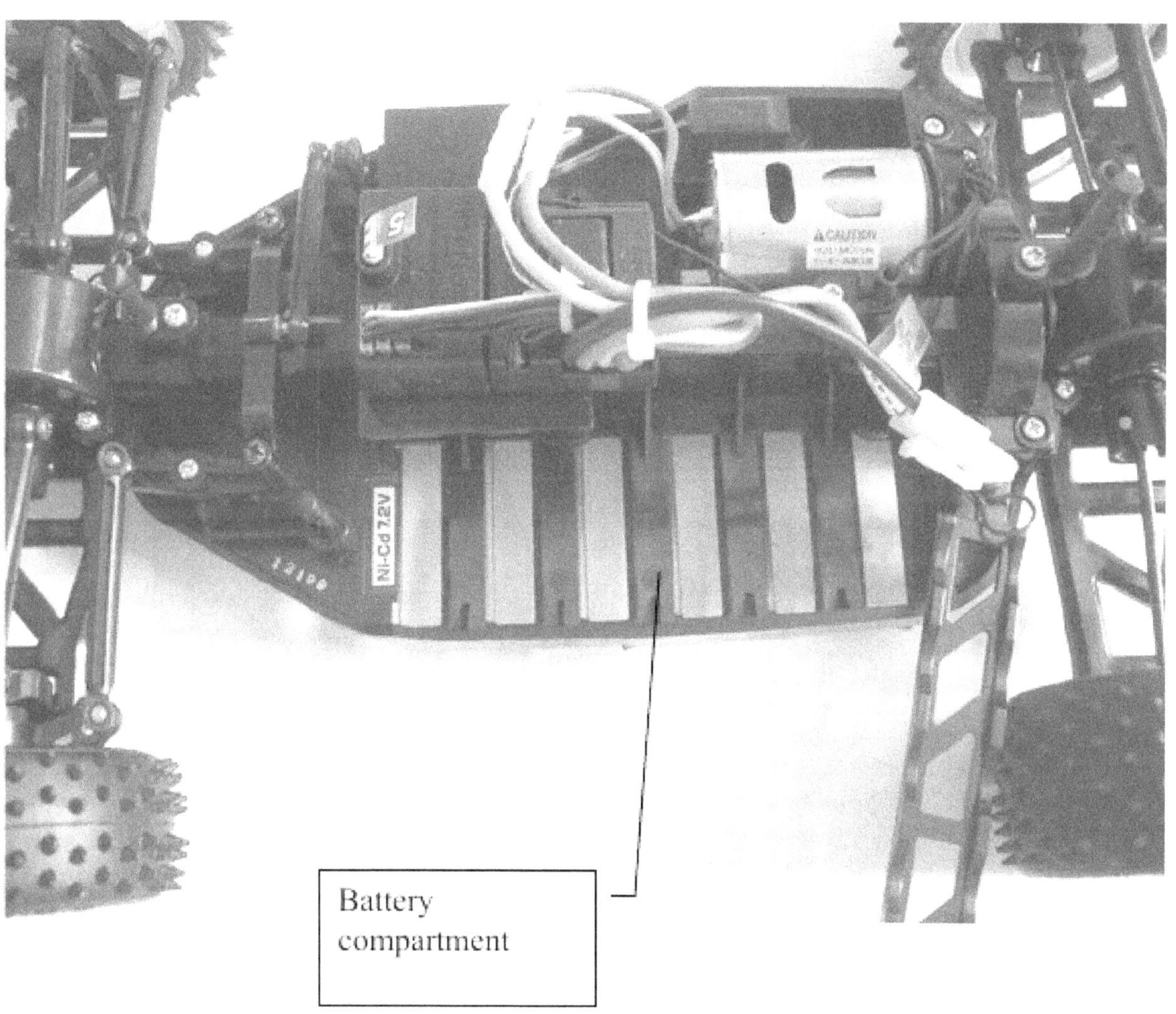

Battery compartment

FYI, standard size 7.2V (or 7.4V with casing) for RC cars should have this dimension: 137mm (Length), 47.5mm (Width), 24mm (Height). Most 1:10 RC car compartments are designed for this size. Some lipo packs may be either too small or too large, which may require that you 3d print special battery compartment. See this example, an alternative battery holder is printed for the Tamiya Wild Dagger (3d print is becoming a MUST if you want to be more serious in RC):

UNDERSTANDING THE RADIO SYSTEM

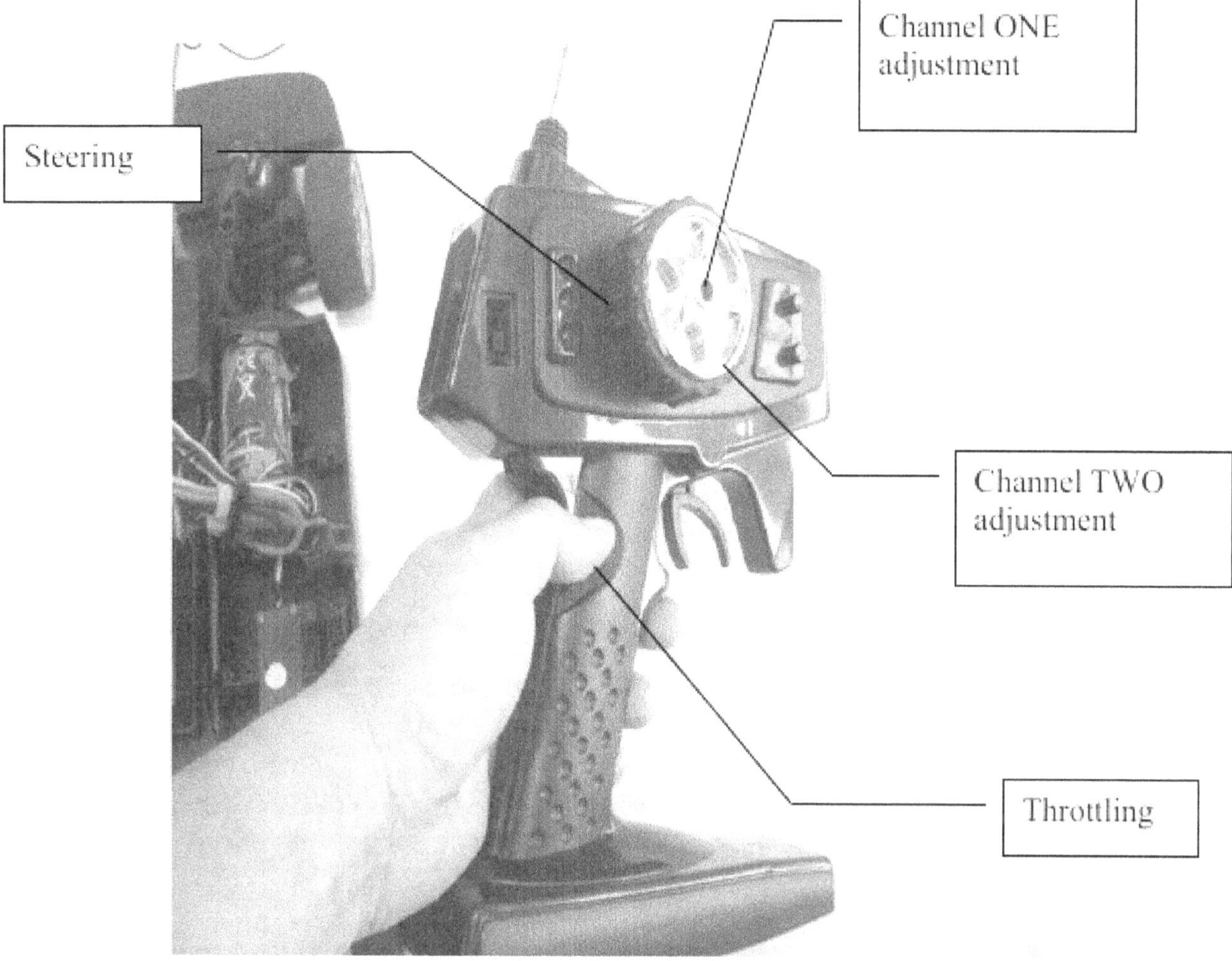

The most popular controller set for RC cars is the wheel-type 2-channel system. With a 2 channel system you can control steering with one channel (channel ONE) and throttling with another (channel TWO). Do note that some legacy AM radio systems may use channel 2 for steering instead. It is really manufacturer-dependent.

In RC terminology, a receiver is an electronic device that receives radio signal from the controller and decodes the signal for controlling the servo and the ESC.

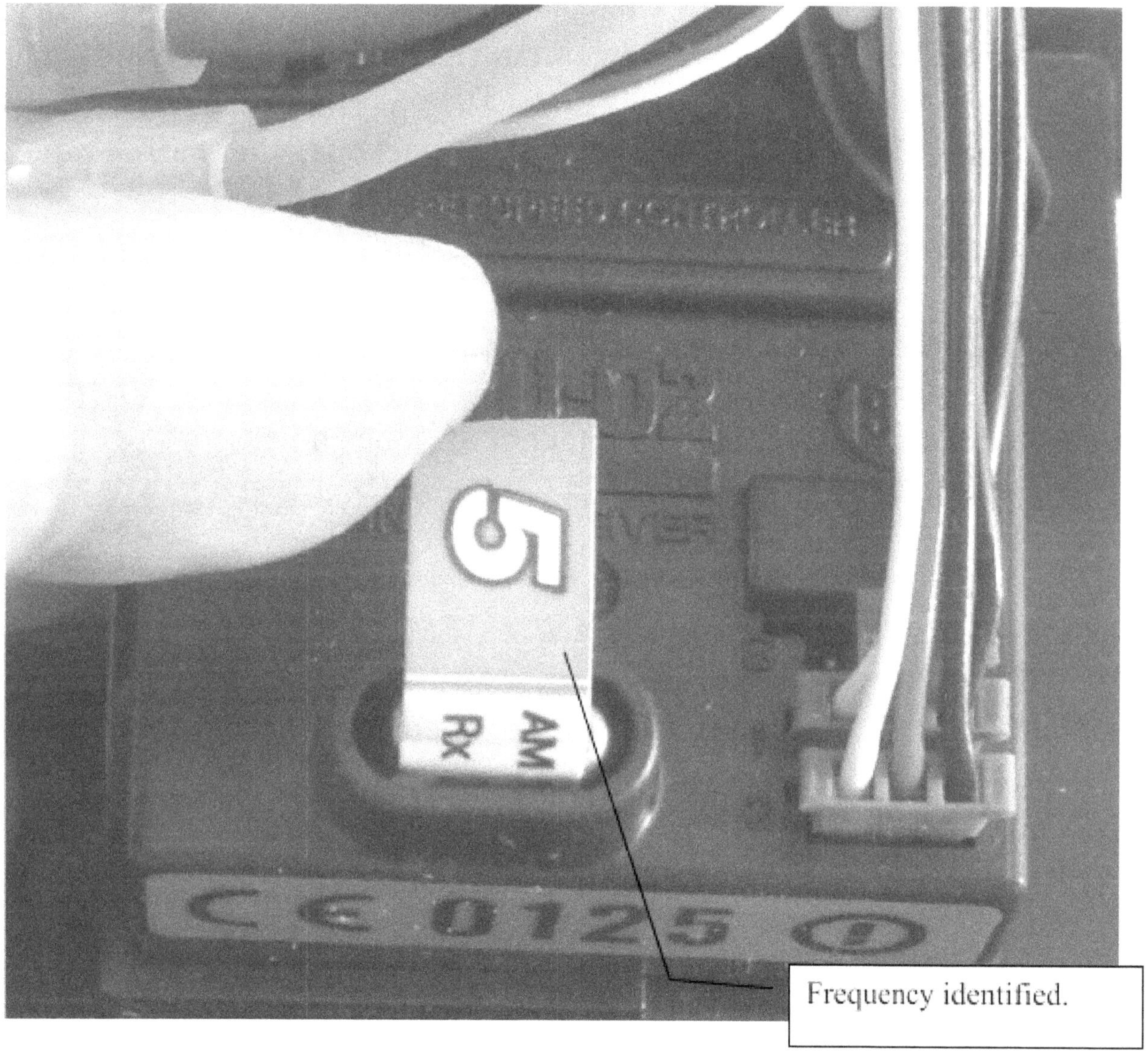

Frequency identified.

You need to know that RC receivers are specific to a given

frequency. The very basic requirement is that the receiver must match the frequency of the radio controller in order to be able to listen to its instructions. Within a frequency channel there are a number of sub frequencies for multiple racers to drive at any given time. If you are buying a RTR package the matching is already done for you. If you are buying these devices separately then you must manually ensure the crystal that is shipped with your receiver is matching the channel of your radio.

Legacy RC radios are either AM or FM based. The crystal is either AM or FM specific and you can tell from the label attached to it. When it says 27mhz it is AM.

If you are using third party ESC and/or servo, you want to ensure the wire plug is compatible. Different brands have different wiring scheme for the plug, so compatibility is not always

guaranteed. Most plugs in the market are Futaba compatible.

Wire plugs (to the ESC and the servo)

A very obvious advantage of deploying 2.4Ghz radio is that you no longer need a very long "antenna" on the car. Also, there are way

more available channels (there are about 80 channels in the

2.4GHz band). In fact, most 2.4G transmitters will automatically

select and lock onto clear channels for you.

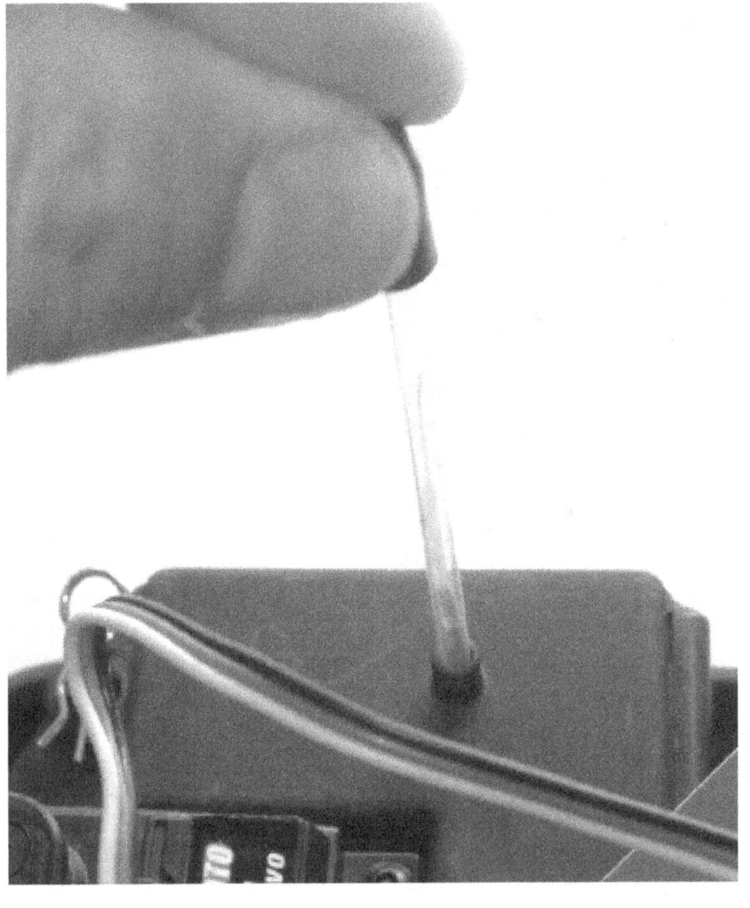

With a 2.4G system, the antenna on the receiving end is very short.

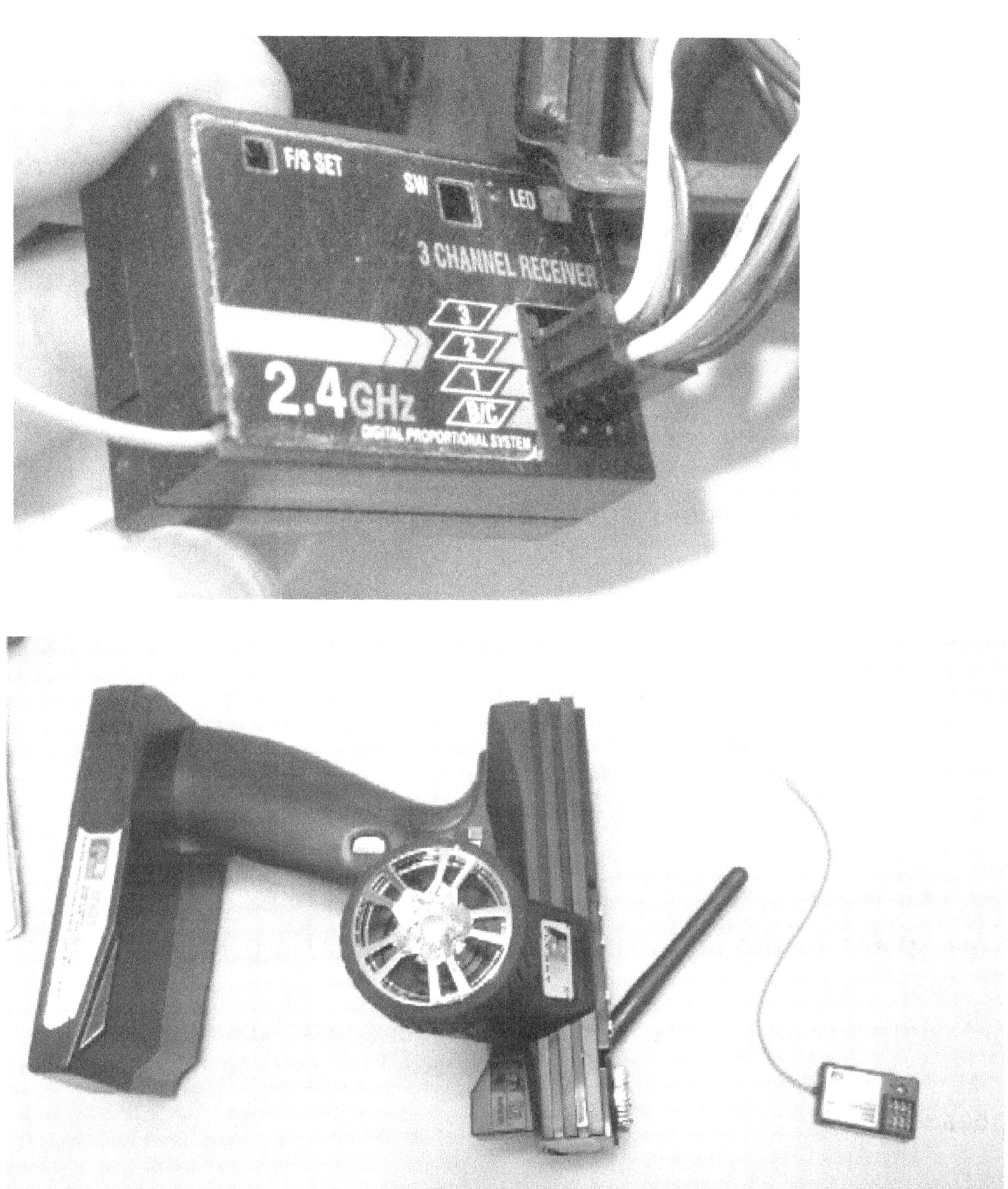
F/S SET
SW
LED
3 CHANNEL RECEIVER
3
2
1
B/C
2.4GHz
DIGITAL PROPORTIONAL SYSTEM

The 2.4G receiver has to work with its own transmitter. You cannot mix and match receiver and transmitter of different brands unless you purchase a receiver specially designed to work with multiple different transmitter models.

Configuration is simple. You turn on the transmitter first and then the ESC. The ESC will immediately supply power to the receiver. The receiver will talk to the transmitter to complete the binding process automatically.

To prevent water and other debris from getting in (receiver is not water-proof), some buggies have a special compartment to house the receiver:

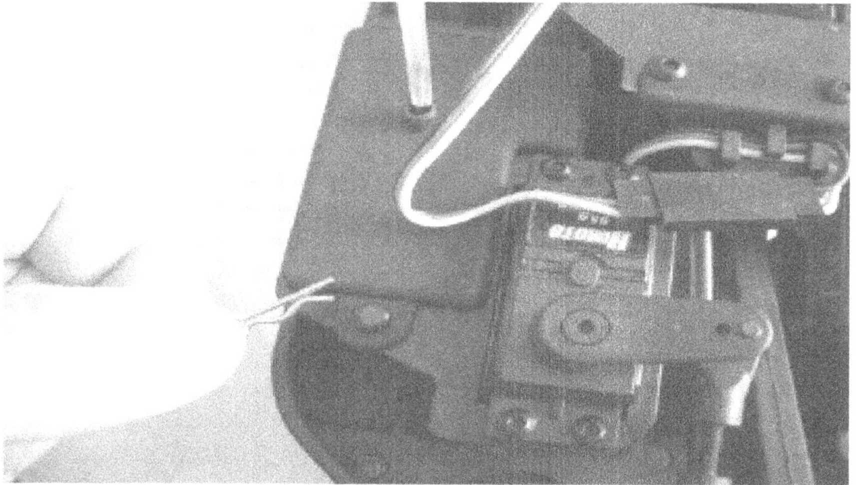

If in case your buggy doesn't have one, a cheaper solution would be to use a balloon to wrap around the receiver.

UNDERSTANDING THE SUSPENSION SYSTEM

The primary components of a suspension system are dampers and stabilizer bars (anti-sway bars). Our demo buggy uses upgrade dampers without sway bars.

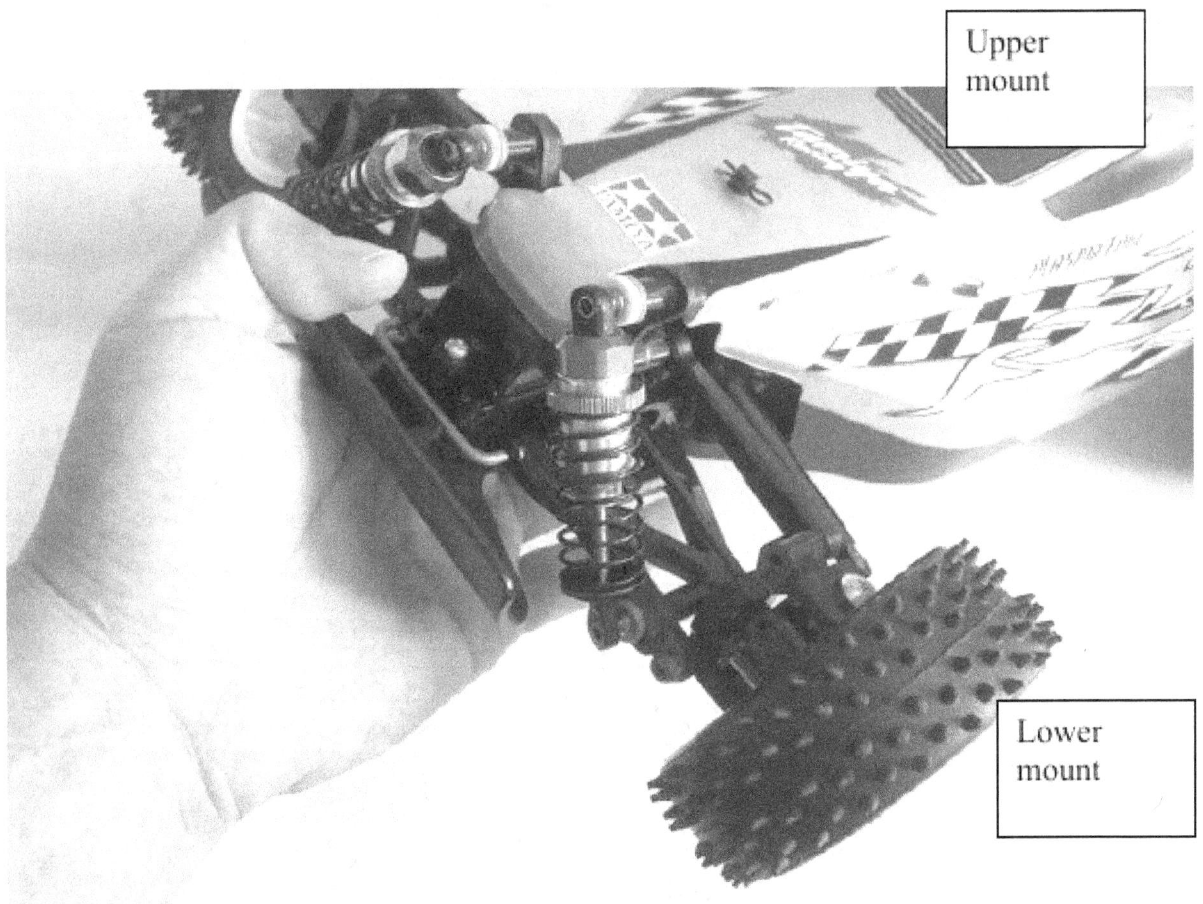

Our demo truck has BOTH deployed.

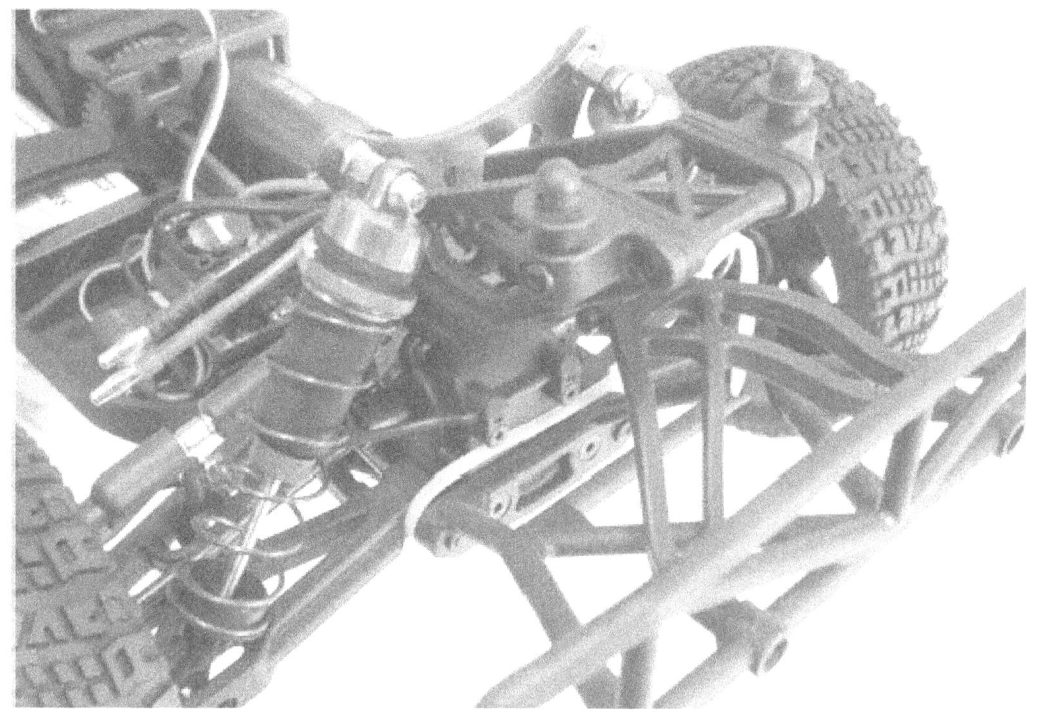

A damper is basically a tube like device placed between the chassis of the buggy and the wheels. The upper mount of the damper connects to the frame, while the lower mount connects to the axle near the wheel.

The 2 major types of RC damper are oil filled shock absorber and pure spring based damper. With a pure spring based damper, you fine tune suspension through adjusting the stiffness of the spring. An oil filled shock absorber, on the other hand, allows for smoother response to differing road conditions through slowing down (smoothing out) the movement of the spring (the "smoothing out" effect can be fine tuned through using different grades of damper oil, which is commonly described by thickness but measured in weight – 10wt is the thinnest while 100wt is the thickest).

Generally speaking, an oil filled shock absorber performs better in terms of road holding and road isolation.

An oil shock absorber has a relatively complicated internal structure with parts like piston, piston rod, valve, pressure tube and cylinder involved, thus leading to a much higher manufacturing cost. It is not unusual for the piston rod of the shock absorber to get oily after a ride or two. Make sure you keep it clean all the time as dirt often likes to stick to the oily surface.

These dampers are oil filled.

Unless there is a serious leak, you shouldn't need to refill it frequently.

Spring adjustment can be achieved through compression adjustment OR spring replacement. The former is less costly.

Metal dampers are stronger – they can normally survive during a crash.

If a pure spring based damper is in use, you may adjust its stiffness through spring replacement or through spring compression with ring type spacers. If an oil filled shock absorber is in use, you may also want to change to a different damper oil or to use travel limiters (which are spacers that come shipped with most absorber kits) to limit the movement of the absorber.

A pure spring based damper

Stabilizer bar (anti-roll / sway bar) can keep the car's body flat by moving force from one side of the body to another, thus reducing the chance of body rolling in a sharp turn (and also reducing the traction you have during a turn). In fact, stabilizer bar packages are usually available as optional upgrade parts in lower cost kits.

One easy way to determine if your existing dampers are too soft for the track is to check the bottom of the chassis after each ride and see if new scratches are popping out all over the place. To determine if proper left/right balance is maintained, see if these scratches are evenly distributed.

A double wishbone suspension has both an upper arm and a lower arm on each side. A single wishbone swing arm design has no upper arm. Instead, a simple rod is used to hold the upright. Our demo cars all use the latter design.

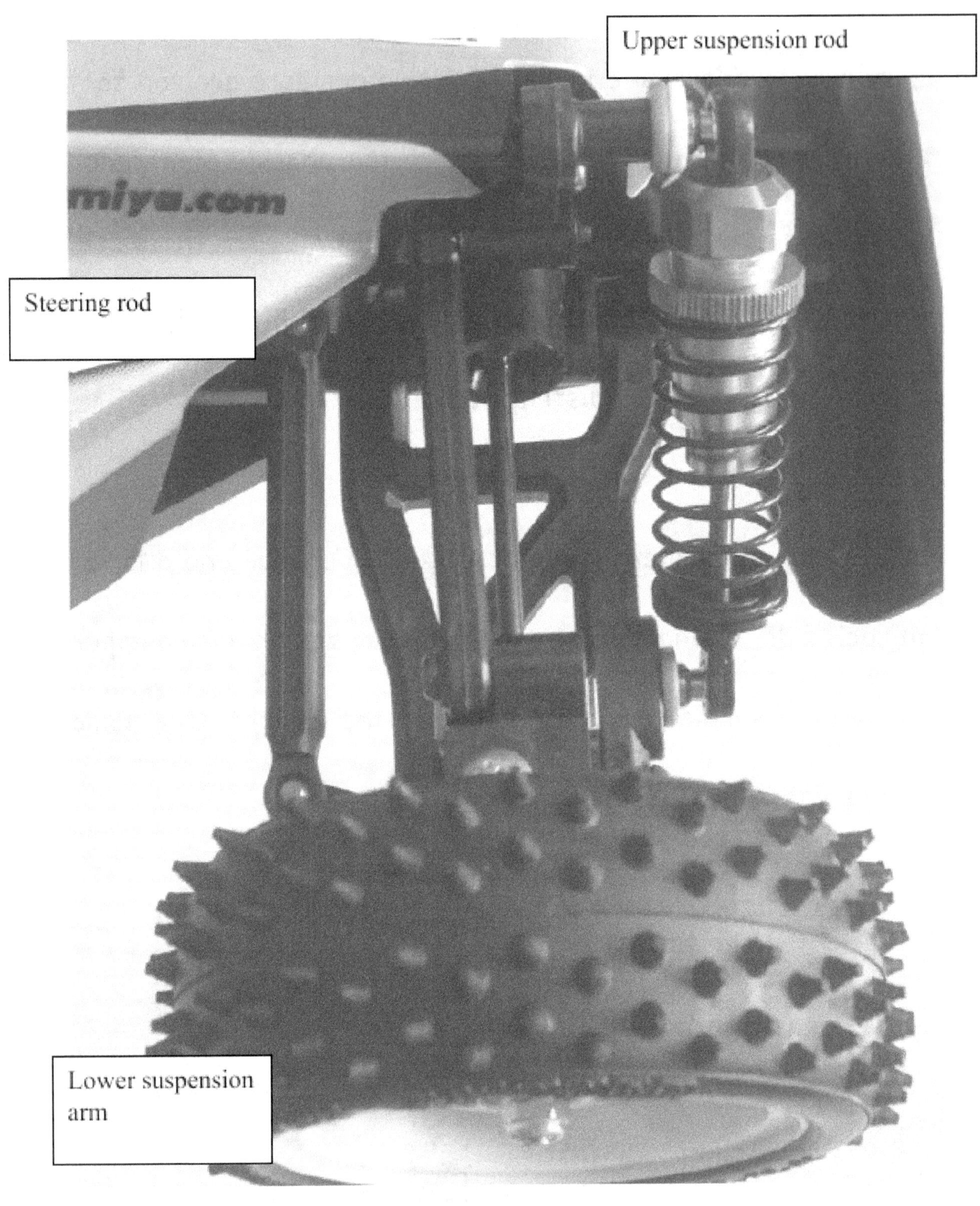
Upper suspension rod
Steering rod
Lower suspension arm
miya.com

TROUBLESHOOTING OFFROAD RC

When there are problems with your offroad cars, several steps can be followed depending on the symptom. The thing is, for troubleshooting to be possible and practical, you often need to have one extra set of spare parts. Successful troubleshooting often involves swapping parts for testing!

If your car does not move at all right from the start, check to see if the car can steer. If the car cannot steer, it is likely that there is no power supplied to the radio system. Something is wrong with the ESC to battery connection, or that the entire radio system is not working. You should try using another battery pack and then another ESC.

If the car can steer, that means the radio is probably working. Now check and see if the ESC-to-receiver connection is right – it should be connected to either channel one or channel two but nothing else.

If ESC-to-receiver is good but the motor does not turn (and you are sure your battery is fully charged), it could be that the motor is bad or the motor pinion is meshing too tight with the spur (the motor is locked up).

Don't mesh the motor pinion gear too close with the spur gear or the motor will have a hard time turning. At the same time, don't mesh them too loose or gear stripping will result. Fine tuning is necessary to get the motor mounted right. When properly set, you should be able to have the wheels spun forward freely and silently.

Try to connect the ESC wires to another motor. Hold the motor by hand and accelerate so to determine if the ESC is actually doing its job. If it does, it is time to take out the motor from the car for inspection. If this motor can spin after getting unmounted, then gear meshing is the problem. If the motor cannot even dry spin, it is dead.

If the car runs for awhile and suddenly stop, first check if it can steer. If steering does not work, either the ESC is dead or the battery is running low so to have triggered the ESC's low voltage protection.

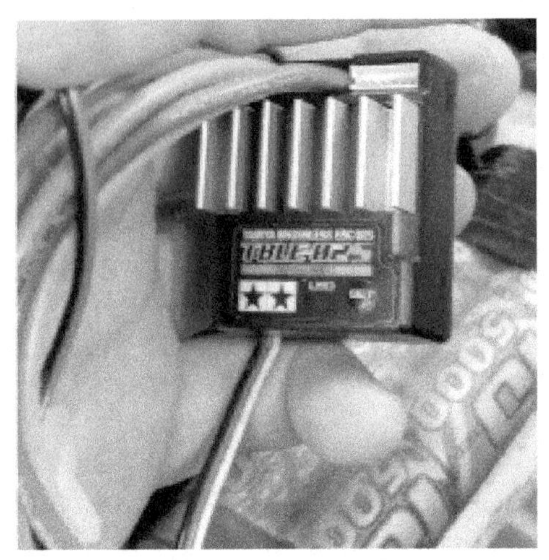

If the ESC is getting damn hot, it could be that thermal protection is in effect. However, if it still doesn't work after it is cooled, it may be something else. It could be that the ESC's on/off switch is bad. Try to remove the switch and have the wires connected directly. If it still doesn't work, you may pretty much conclude that the ESC is dead. BTW, check the manual of the ESC and see if there is any indication that can be observed from the LED.

If the ESC appears to work hard pushing the motor (the led light is on and you hear some strange noise from the motor), it could be that something gets in the way of any of the wheels or dog bone shafts, effectively preventing the drive train from working properly.

If your motor is a brushed one and there is an internal fan inside, that fan can deform due to excessive heat and stop the motor from working. Your motor can get overheated if meshing is too tight or that the pinion gear you use is too large (large pinion can increase workload significantly). The ESC's thermal protection function cannot detect heat on the motor and would not cut off power when the motor is cooking itself.

If the car is moving but steering becomes unresponsive, it could be that something is wrong with the servo saver (if there is one), or the servo is dead.

The whole point of using a servo saver is to protect the servo from gear breakage during a crash. The C shape plastic (the C ring) of the servo saver takes the hit and gets cracked. The problem is that if it is too soft, the servo may have a hard time centering back after a steer. If the C ring is broken, steering may fail entirely. As a quick fix on the field you may try to use a zip tie to tighten it up.

Also check and see if there are wires that get in the way of the servo horn. If so, use zip ties to organize the wires in a proper way.

If you have dropped your transmitter on the ground before, it could be that the internal connection of the steering wheel is loose. Test the car using another transmitter (if you have one) to confirm this.

If the car moves but with strange noise along the way, it could be that motor mounting is loose so the pinion is moving away from the spur. If your car is a belt car, it could be that something gets into the drive train scratching the belt. In any case you should always keep your drive train properly sealed in an offroad environment!

If your car suddenly fails to go straight but there is nothing wrong with the servo or the servo saver, check the dog bone shafts at the front. It could be that one of them is already missing! A shaft dropped on grassland is almost always gone forever...

Universal shaft has one end permanently attached to the hub so you won't lose it... This is an upgrade option that is definitely worth your consideration if you always run your car on grassland.

If the car runs noisily, apply silicon spray onto the bearings of all wheels, shafts and hubs. Also apply some on the bearings of the motor. For spur gear and pinion gear, apply grease. Avoid WD40 since it is corrosive on plastics.

Grassland with thick grass can easily kill your motor and your ESC. Grassland with thin grass, on the other hand, is more appropriate.

Changing to larger wheels without upgrading the motor or changing the gear ratio may lead to overheat too. For example, when you fit a Stadium Raider with some larger wheels, you can turn it into a monster truck like vehicle.

However, since this car does not have much flexibility in changing the gears, you should upgrade the motor to one with higher torque. A regular 540 silver can may not have the torque to survive. 550 is for sure better. In fact, most 550 variations can survive 3S power! If your ESC can handle 3S, it would not hurt to try 3S! 3S rocks (if the chassis is strong enough for the increased stress – 3S runs and jumps with crazy horsepower)!

Latest 2025 Information Update

Motor above 27T

The standard Silver Can 540 from Mabuchi is 27T. The Team Power black motor is 23T. Johnson Electric's 540 silver can (with white plastic cap) is between 21-23T.

On the market there are quite many brushed motors that are 35T or above.

"35T" means 35 turns of wire in the motor's armature. Generally, higher turn count = more torque, less speed. A 35T motor offers a balance:

- More torque than a 27T (better for climbing and rough terrain).
- More speed than a 45T or 55T (less sluggish on trails).
- Perfect for general off-road driving with some crawling.

Because 35T motors spin more slowly and draw less current than lower-turn motors (like 12T or 15T, which are designed for speed), they typically run cooler under normal conditions. This makes them ideal for crawling and technical terrain where smooth throttle control and consistent torque are more important than raw speed.

That said, overheating is still possible under certain conditions. If you:

- Overgear the vehicle (using too large a pinion gear),
- Run it in deep grass or sand that strains the drivetrain,
- Block airflow,
- Or apply constant throttle under heavy loads for long periods,

You can still cause heat buildup. Heat issues can also arise from poor maintenance, like worn brushes, dirty commutators, or binding in the drivetrain. HOWEVER, in normal use—particularly in slow, torque-heavy applications—a 35T brushed motor is reliable and runs cool, making it a favorite for scale and crawler setups where overheating is rarely a concern. 50T should be even better in this regard.

The reason 35T, 50T, and other high-turn motors are almost always brushed rather than brushless is mostly about simplicity, low-speed control, and application. These motors are most often used in crawlers, trail trucks, and scale vehicles—situations where torque, smooth throttle response, and fine control at low RPMs are more important than raw speed or efficiency. Brushed motors naturally provide excellent low-end torque and linear throttle feel, which makes them ideal for slow, technical driving. High-turn brushed motors spin slowly, offering more torque and precision, and they're mechanically simple, inexpensive, and very reliable in dusty or wet environments. For applications like the scale rock crawlers, this makes them the go-to choice.

Brushless motors, on the other hand, tend to excel in speed-focused applications. While you can get brushless motors that emulate the slow, torquey behavior of high-turn brushed motors (using sensored systems and specific tuning), they are usually more expensive, require a compatible ESC, and still don't always match the same crawl-friendly feel of a good brushed setup. Also, brushless motors don't use "turns" in the same direct way—turn count means something different between brushed and brushless systems—so you won't typically see brushless motors labeled as 50T or 60T.

Sensored or sensorless?

Choosing between a sensored and a sensorless brushless motor depends on the specific application and priorities—mainly around smoothness, control, complexity, and cost. A sensored brushless motor has built-in sensors (usually Hall effect sensors) that monitor the rotor's position and feed that information to the ESC. This allows for extremely smooth and precise control, especially at low speeds. As a result, sensored systems excel in applications like rock crawling, drifting, or racing, where throttle precision and consistent power delivery are critical. They offer smoother startup, zero cogging at low RPM, and better throttle response under load. However, they are typically more expensive, and the sensor cables add a layer of complexity and vulnerability—if the sensor wire becomes damaged or disconnected, the motor can lose its smoothness or fail to operate correctly.

In contrast, a sensorless brushless motor operates without knowing the rotor's exact position. Instead, it estimates this based on the back-EMF (voltage generated by the spinning motor) once it gets moving. This makes the system simpler, cheaper, and more robust—there are fewer wires and no sensor to damage. Sensorless motors are often used in high-speed applications like buggies, monster trucks, or boats, where precise low-end control is less important, and top-end efficiency and power are prioritized. The downside is rougher startup, especially under load, and less consistent throttle control at low speeds, which can cause cogging (a stuttering or hesitation).

Ultimately, if you prioritize low-speed control, smooth startup, and precision driving, such as in crawling or on-road racing, a sensored motor is the better choice. But if you're more focused on simplicity, durability, and high-speed performance, and you're willing to accept less finesse at low RPMs, then a sensorless motor may be the smarter and more cost-effective option.

Differentials and One way

In the past, ball differentials were the standard choice for high-performance touring cars and buggies. They worked by using small steel balls running between pressure plates, allowing the driver to fine-tune the differential action by tightening or loosening a single screw. This gave a very smooth, connected feel to the car, ideal for technical tracks where subtle control was key. However, as racing technology evolved, gear differentials began to replace ball diffs as the preferred option. One major reason for this shift is consistency. Ball differentials naturally wear during a run, as the balls and plates heat up and slowly polish each other down. This can cause the differential setting to change mid-race, leading to unpredictable handling. Gear differentials, by contrast, maintain their performance lap after lap, especially when filled with the right silicone oil. This stability makes it easier for drivers to push the car with confidence.

Durability is another big factor. Ball diffs are somewhat fragile, especially when subjected to the violent forces generated by today's powerful brushless motors and high-grip racing surfaces. It's common for a ball diff to slip, flatten the balls, or even explode under heavy loads. Gear diffs, with their solid internal gears and oil cushioning, can handle much greater stress without breaking down. Another advantage is the range and precision of tuning. While a ball diff's action is adjusted by mechanical tension, a gear diff can be tuned more easily and more predictably by simply changing the weight of the silicone oil inside. Light oils allow for easy cornering with plenty of differentiation, while heavier oils can simulate a nearly locked diff, offering incredible drive out of corners. This flexibility makes gear diffs much easier to match to different tracks and driving styles.

The move toward gear diffs was also helped by changes in racing environments. Modern on-road tracks, especially carpet tracks, now offer much higher levels of grip than they did 20 years ago. On these surfaces, a ball diff can struggle to stay planted and often slips under sudden loads, while a gear diff maintains traction more reliably.

Finally, ease of maintenance has also pushed racers toward gear diffs. Maintaining a ball differential requires careful disassembly, cleaning, and precise reassembly to keep it performing at its best. In contrast, gear diffs are simple: a basic teardown and oil refill are enough to keep them running strong, even across multiple race days.

In short, racers today prefer gear differentials because they offer greater durability, more consistent performance, easier tuning, and less maintenance. Although ball diffs still have their uses in certain classes and conditions, for most modern RC racing applications, gear diffs have simply become the smarter, more competitive choice.

A one-way bearing, often just called a "one-way," changes the way the drivetrain behaves, especially under braking and cornering, and it can have a big impact on how the car handles.

The Yokomo Re Release 834B has it. Some other high performance cars also do.

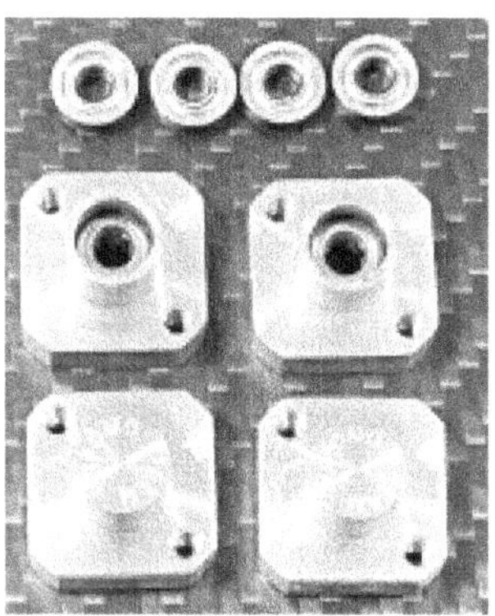

At its core, the one-way bearing lets the front wheels spin freely forward without resistance when they're not being powered. Under acceleration, it locks up and transmits full power to the front wheels like normal, so you still get all-wheel drive traction. But when you come off the throttle or start braking, the one-way unlocks, and the front wheels are no longer mechanically connected to the motor or brakes. They just coast independently. This has a few really interesting effects. First, when you're braking, only the rear wheels are actually being slowed by the motor or by any electronic brake force from the ESC. The front wheels are left free to roll, which means the car can rotate into a corner more aggressively. Instead of the whole car slowing down evenly and staying super stable, the rear end slows down more than the front, which tends to loosen up the back and make the car turn in sharper. In racing terms, it gives you much stronger initial turn-in and can make the car feel a lot more nimble and "pointy" when you dive into corners. However, it's not without downsides. Because you lose braking at the front wheels, overall braking power is reduced. If you're not careful, you can easily lock up the rear tires, causing the car to spin out under hard braking. On high-grip tracks with skilled driving, that aggressive rotation can be an advantage, but on low-grip surfaces or when you need strong straight-line braking, a one-way can make the car much harder to drive. You also have less stability coming into corners, because the front isn't helping slow the car down and keep it straight.

Another thing that happens with a one-way is that if you lift off the throttle suddenly mid-corner, the car doesn't drag the front end down — the front keeps rolling freely, so the car can stay more balanced through fast sweepers. It's a totally different feel compared to a regular center differential or solid drive setup where the front end is always being slowed mechanically.

Back in the heyday of touring car racing, one-ways were really popular because they helped carry more corner speed and made cars super quick in and out of turns. But they eventually fell out of favor for most drivers because of the extra difficulty managing braking and the inconsistency they introduced, especially on rougher or dustier tracks.

Installing a one-way is kind of a commitment — it changes the way you have to drive. You usually need to brake earlier and more gently, and you steer the car more with throttle control than by jamming on the brakes. It's one of those tuning options that, in the right hands and the right conditions, can be magic, but for casual driving or rough surfaces, it's often better to stick with a center diff or a spool. The one-way differential is a bit more complex. It's a full front differential that has one-way bearings built into it, typically connected to the outdrives or internal gears. Under acceleration, it acts like a locked axle or solid diff — delivering power evenly to both front wheels for maximum traction and drive. But under braking or coasting, the one-way bearings allow each front wheel to spin independently. This gives you a differential effect under braking, which can help the car stay more stable and maintain better control because the front wheels can rotate at different speeds, matching whatever grip they find. In a way, it's more refined: you still get a sharp front-end feeling like with a simple one-way bearing setup, but the car doesn't become quite as "knife-edge" or unstable under braking. The main difference, really, is that the one-way bearing affects the entire front drivetrain in a very binary way — fully locked when on throttle, fully free when off. Meanwhile, the one-way differential offers a more dynamic behavior by allowing each front wheel to behave independently under certain conditions, giving you a blend of sharp turn-in and braking stability. In practice, a simple one-way bearing is more aggressive and can make the car faster if you can handle it, but harder to drive. A one-way differential is more forgiving, smoother, and often better suited for tracks that aren't perfectly flat or ultra high-grip. It sort of comes down to whether you want a full "race knife" feel (one-way bearing) or a more nuanced, balanced behavior (one-way differential).

The one way diff unit assembly for Tamiya:

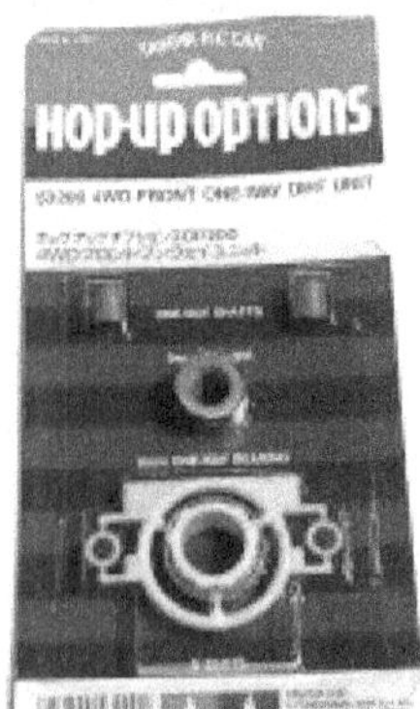

Gear ratio change VS motor upgrade

When you're choosing between changing the gear ratio or installing a faster motor, you're essentially picking between two different strategies for improving speed, each with its own advantages and trade-offs.

If you change the gear ratio — for example, by fitting a larger pinion gear or a smaller spur gear — you effectively make the car geared for higher top speeds. The main pro here is efficiency. You're still using the same motor and electronic setup, just making the drivetrain better suited for speed rather than torque. This often costs very little (just the gears themselves) and doesn't require significant rework of your car's internals. However, the downside is that you will lose acceleration and torque. The car might become slower off the line and may struggle more on hills, rough terrain, or if you're running on anything other than smooth flat surfaces. It could also cause the motor to run hotter, because it's working harder at low speeds to move the car.

Not all cars give you the luxury to change gears though. Lower end offroad cars are quite limited in the choice of spur gear and motor pinion. Now, if you swap to a faster motor without changing gears, the effect is different. A motor with a higher Kv rating (more RPM per volt) will spin faster for the same voltage, giving you more top-end speed even without touching the gears. The benefit here is that you often get both better speed and maintain relatively decent acceleration, depending on how big a change you make. Faster motors can deliver more power and sometimes better throttle response too. But, the big cons are heat and efficiency: higher Kv motors usually draw more current, which can overstress your ESC and battery. They also tend to have less torque unless you pair them with different gearing. Plus, upgrading a motor is often more expensive than simply swapping gears, and you might need to upgrade supporting components (ESC, better cooling fans, stronger batteries) to handle the increased demand. The thing is, if your car model does not have the flexibility needed for changing gears, using faster motor would become the only possible choice.

Would you be doing this for casual bashing, racing, or something else? That could swing the best choice too.

Slipper clutch

The slipper clutch in an electric RC car plays a really interesting and important role, especially when you're dealing with high-powered setups or running off-road.

You can find slipper clutch on higher end cars such as those from Team Associate, HPI, Traxxas ....etc.

The Slipper clutch assembly for HPI:

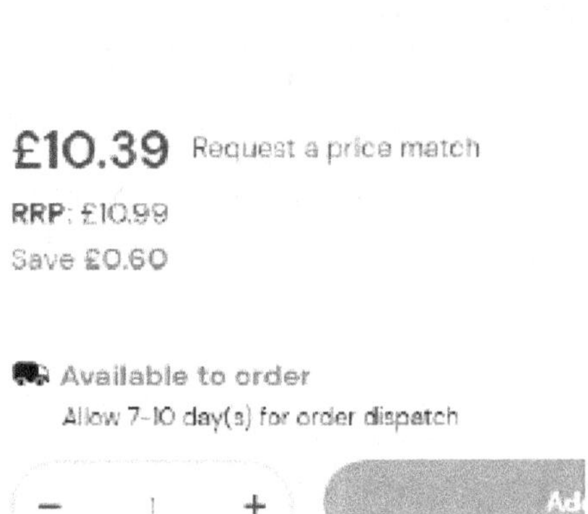

At its core, a slipper clutch is built into the transmission and is designed to allow a little bit of controlled slipping between the motor's output and the wheels. This happens mainly when there's a sudden load or shock — like when you land a jump, hit a bump, or nail the throttle too hard from a standstill. Instead of transferring all that force directly to the drivetrain, which could easily break gears, snap drive shafts, or just make the car hard to control, the slipper clutch slips just enough to absorb the impact and smooth things out.

Mechanically, it usually consists of a spur gear sandwiched between friction pads and a pressure plate. A spring-loaded nut or a similar tensioner system controls how tightly everything is pressed together. When you tighten the slipper, it allows less slip and transfers more direct power to the wheels. When you loosen it, it lets the clutch slip more easily under heavy load, softening the hit to the drivetrain and smoothing out traction.

The Slipper clutch assembly for Traxxas Slash and Stampede:

From a handling perspective, it can help a lot with traction too. On loose dirt or gravel, for instance, if you have too much direct power, you'll just spin the wheels and lose control. A properly adjusted slipper clutch can help "meter" that initial burst of power, letting the wheels hook up better instead of lighting up uselessly. It's particularly useful in 2WD cars, where sudden bursts of torque can make the car fishtail or spin out very easily.

That said, setting the slipper clutch properly is key. If it's too loose, you waste power and the car will feel sluggish off the line, almost like the motor is revving without moving the car properly. If it's too tight, you might as well not have a slipper at all, and you risk damaging the drivetrain if you hit something or get a wheel stuck. It's a balance — enough slip to protect the mechanical parts and improve control, but tight enough to efficiently put down the power when you want it.

Tuning a slipper clutch is actually one of those little rituals that makes you feel really connected to your RC car once you get the hang of it. First, you start by tightening the slipper clutch all the way down — but not crazy tight, just firm enough that the spring is fully compressed and there's no slipping at all. This basically locks it out temporarily. Then, you back it off — usually about a quarter to half a turn. The exact amount depends on your car, motor power, and surface conditions, but that's a good starting point.

Once you have it set, you place the car on a high-traction surface (like clean concrete or asphalt) and do a punch test. This is where you give it full throttle from a dead stop. You're watching — and listening — for what happens in the first split-second. If the front of the car pops up or the rear tires break loose and spin violently, the slipper might be too tight. If the car launches smoothly but with a slight "slip" sound before taking off, that's usually perfect.

On the other hand, if you hear a lot of high-pitched slipping noise and the car feels lazy, then it's too loose — you tighten it a little and test again. If it launches like a cannon and your tires balloon or your car squirms badly, it's too tight — you loosen it a little and try again.

Some racers also like to hold the rear tires firmly while giving a little throttle and feeling how much the slipper gives. You don't want the motor to overpower your grip easily, but you do want it to feel like it's breaking free slightly if you really hold firm. The key is tuning it not just for pure launch power, but for consistent control. On high-grip surfaces you can run a tighter slipper because there's less wheel spin. On loose, dusty tracks, you'll usually want it looser to avoid just blowing away traction at launch. And in bashing situations, where big jumps and crash landings are common, you might even favor a slightly looser slipper to help protect the transmission when the tires hit the ground spinning. It's one of those adjustments you kind of "feel" your way into, and after a while, your ears and fingers will know when it's just right.

Anti-Roll

The anti-roll bar, often called a sway bar, in an electric RC car works similarly to the ones you find in full-sized cars, and it's all about controlling body roll during cornering to make the car more stable and predictable.

This Yokomo 834B has anti roll at the rear end:

Mechanically, it's a simple but clever setup. You have a metal rod, usually mounted across the chassis, that connects the left and right suspension arms. When the car is driving in a straight line and both wheels are moving up and down evenly, the bar doesn't really do anything. It just sits there, basically passive. But when you turn and the car starts to lean — where one side's suspension compresses and the other side extends — that's when the bar kicks in. As one side of the suspension moves up, the bar resists twisting, and this resistance tries to push down on the opposite side, counteracting the rolling motion of the chassis.

The effect of this is that it keeps the car flatter through corners. A flatter car usually means the tires stay more evenly loaded, and you maintain better traction. It also makes the handling feel tighter and more responsive. Without this bar, especially on a car with a soft suspension setup, the chassis would lean heavily into turns, unloading the inside wheels, making the car feel sloppy, unpredictable, and more likely to traction-roll (flip over sideways).

What's interesting is that by adjusting the stiffness of the bar — either by swapping to a thicker or thinner bar, or by tweaking how it's mounted — you can fine-tune the handling balance. A stiffer front bar generally makes the car understeer more, meaning it pushes wide in corners, because it reduces front grip relative to the rear. A stiffer rear bar tends to do the opposite — it can cause oversteer, where the rear end wants to step out during a turn. Racers will often tune their sway bars depending on track conditions: grippier tracks might call for a stiffer bar to control chassis roll, while loose or bumpy tracks might benefit from softer bars or no bars at all to let the suspension work more independently.

One thing to keep in mind is that while these bars improve handling precision, they can also reduce the amount of independent suspension movement. On rough terrain, that can actually hurt grip, because you want each wheel to be able to move up and down as freely as possible without affecting the other side. That's why off-road buggies and trucks often run lighter or no sway bars compared to on-road touring cars where surface smoothness and precision matter most.

When you change the damper settings on your car — meaning making the shocks softer or harder — you're really tuning how the car reacts to bumps, weight transfer, and general handling balance. Softer dampers, whether at the front, the rear, or both, will always allow the suspension to move more easily and soak up more bumps, but where you soften them changes very different aspects of the car's behavior.

If you soften only the front dampers, the front of the car becomes more compliant. It will dive more under braking, meaning the nose will drop down quicker when you get off the throttle or hit the brakes. In corners, the softer front will also let the front tires stay in contact with the ground better over small bumps and rough patches, which can improve front-end grip. The car will typically feel like it wants to "turn in" better because the weight shifts onto the front tires more effectively, giving you sharper steering. However, if you go too soft, it can make the car a little twitchy or nervous because the front will react very quickly and sometimes too much to every input or bump. On the other hand, if you soften only the rear dampers, it's the rear that becomes more lively. The rear of the car will squat more under acceleration — when you hit the throttle, the back end will compress more easily, helping to plant the rear tires for better traction. In corners, a softer rear can also improve grip on bumpy surfaces because the rear wheels will track the ground more faithfully. But the downside is that you may introduce more body roll, and if the rear gets too soft compared to the front, it can cause understeer — where the front turns but the rear doesn't follow cleanly, and the car pushes wide through turns.

If you soften both the front and rear dampers, you make the entire car generally softer and more compliant. This is often great for rough or bumpy tracks because the whole chassis can better absorb terrain changes, keeping more consistent tire contact. The car will roll more in corners, weight transfer will be more pronounced, and everything will happen a little more slowly. This can actually make the car feel easier to drive because it reacts less abruptly to sudden inputs. However, the tradeoff is that it might feel sluggish on smooth, high-grip tracks, and it can be harder to maintain tight, aggressive lines because the car takes longer to settle after every bump or steering input.

Comparing the three: softening only the front generally gives you better steering but risks twitchiness; softening only the rear gives you more traction and stability but can reduce steering sharpness; softening both gives you better overall bump absorption but at the cost of precision and crisp handling. In reality, tuning dampers is really about matching your suspension reaction speed to the surface and your driving style. Smooth track? Probably want stiffer dampers. Rough track? Softer dampers let the car flow better over the surface.

Why NOT use WD-40 for lubing gears?

It's not a good idea to use WD-40 on RC car gears if you're thinking about proper lubrication for running the car.

WD-40 is mainly a water-displacer and light cleaner, not a proper lubricant for gears. When you spray it onto gears, it gives them a bit of slickness at first, but it doesn't last under high-speed loads. Worse, it actually washes away any real grease that might have been there before. After it evaporates — and it does evaporate pretty fast — you're left with almost no protection. The gears are then exposed to metal-on-metal contact, which leads to wear, grinding, and potential gear failure over time. On top of that, WD-40 tends to attract dirt and dust, especially on exposed gears like spur gears and pinions, and when that happens, it forms a kind of gritty paste that can absolutely wreck your drivetrain.

Now, if you're just cleaning gears — like after running through mud or water — you could use WD-40 as a temporary cleaner to flush dirt and moisture off. But you should always wipe it dry afterward and reapply proper lubricant before using the car again.

For plastic gears (like on many Tamiya or budget RCs), you should use a silicone grease. It's safe for plastic and won't degrade the material. For metal gears (like in high-end buggies, truggies, or crawlers), you should use molybdenum grease, lithium grease, or specific RC gear grease made for high-pressure applications. These greases stay where they're needed and form a protective, lasting barrier under hard use. For open spur and pinion gears, especially in on-road racing where you want things to spin really freely, many racers actually run them dry or use a very light dry lube (like graphite spray) to avoid dirt sticking. But in most bashing or off-road cars, a little proper grease is better to protect the teeth. There are also brands that make RC-specific lubricants — like Tamiya Ceramic Grease, Team Associated Black Grease, or Traxxas High-Performance Grease — which are all designed for this exact kind of work.

Choice of screws: Hex VS Philips

People prefer hex screws over Phillips screws in RC cars because hex screws are way tougher, more reliable, and easier to work with under the kinds of stresses and precision that RC cars demand. The biggest thing is stripping. Phillips screws are designed in a way that the tool is supposed to "cam out" — meaning the screwdriver is *meant* to slip out of the screw head once it gets tight enough. This is actually intentional in a lot of full-size products to avoid over-tightening. But on an RC car, that's exactly what you *don't* want. You're often tightening screws into metal, plastic, or tiny threaded inserts, and when the screwdriver slips out of a Phillips screw head, it strips the cross slots. Once it's stripped, it becomes a nightmare — you can't tighten it properly, and worse, it becomes almost impossible to remove later. And because RC screws are tiny, stripping them is very easy with Phillips heads.

Hex screws, on the other hand, have a deep hexagonal socket that matches the tip of an Allen wrench perfectly. When you tighten or loosen a hex screw, the tool stays engaged without slipping. This means you can apply much more torque without fear of stripping, and if you ever need to remove them after a hard crash, rough run, or muddy race, they're much easier to deal with. Plus, when you use good quality tools (like hardened steel Allen drivers), the feel and precision are way better. Another reason is wear and longevity. Phillips screws and tools wear out faster. Over time, your screwdriver tip gets rounded off, making it even easier to strip heads. Good hex drivers last much longer, and they give you a crisper fit for a lot longer. Also, assembly and maintenance speed matters. In racing, when you need to fix something quickly between heats, hex screws make it faster and less risky. You can spin them in and out quickly with electric screwdrivers fitted with hex bits, and they won't slip like Phillips often do.

A lot of modern RC kits — especially higher-end brands like Team Associated, TLR, Xray, Tekno, etc. — ship with hex hardware from the start because it's basically considered the proper standard now. Phillips screws are mostly still seen on cheaper, entry-level kits, toy-grade cars, or older designs. One more little thing: hex screws just look cleaner and more professional on a car. They fit with the vibe of a serious, race-ready machine.

Choices of chassis material: Nylon VS ABS

Nylon-based plastic is indeed quite common in RC cars nowadays, and it's used for parts where strength, flexibility, and impact resistance are crucial, like in suspension arms, gears, and certain chassis components. Nylon, which can also be referred to as polyamide, is known for its high durability, good wear resistance, and toughness under stress. It's a great choice for parts that need to withstand shocks, flex, and overall rough handling — which is exactly what happens in an RC car during bashing or off-road racing. In contrast, ABS (Acrylonitrile Butadiene Styrene) is known for its rigidity, stability, and ease of molding. It is typically used in parts like bodies, frame structures, and some internal components. The main difference is that ABS is stiffer and more impact-resistant in a way that is suited for parts that need to keep their shape and handle occasional impacts without cracking.

Comparison of Nylon and ABS:

- Appearance: ABS usually gives a more shiny, glossy surface than nylon. If you look at an unpainted Tamiya body accessory or a plastic bumper mount, it often has a clean, semi-gloss shine straight out of the mold. Nylon, on the other hand, is more fibrous and slightly porous at a microscopic level. Even when injection-molded smoothly, it usually looks more matte or semi-matte. Nylon tends to absorb a little bit of moisture from the air (it's hygroscopic), which also contributes to a slightly softer, duller surface appearance. It's incredibly tough and flexible — great for gears, arms, or parts that take impacts — but it doesn't have the crisp, shiny finish that ABS can achieve.
- Strength and Durability: Nylon generally wins in terms of strength and flexibility, especially under dynamic loads. It has higher tensile strength and better wear resistance, which makes it ideal for moving parts like suspension arms or gears. Nylon also has self-lubricating properties, meaning it's less likely to wear out due to friction. ABS, on the other hand, is stronger in terms of rigidity but tends to be more brittle under high-impact situations. It's better for parts that don't need to bend or flex much, like the car body or structural elements that should retain their shape. In extreme stress or impacts (like crashing into a wall), ABS can crack or shatter, whereas nylon will usually bend without breaking.
- Flexibility and Impact Resistance: Nylon shines here — it's more flexible than ABS and can take impacts without cracking. So, for parts that are going to take a lot of rough handling, nylon is the better choice. Think about parts like suspension arms or gears; they need to absorb shocks and flex under stress without snapping. ABS, though, is more rigid and better at maintaining its form over time. But in terms of crash resilience, nylon handles that kind of stress better than ABS does. ABS tends to be more rigid and while it resists scratching and fading over time, it doesn't handle twisting or bending as well under heavy loads.

- Weight: Nylon is slightly heavier than ABS due to its toughness and density. This can be a factor in the overall performance, especially in racing scenarios where weight reduction is key. However, in many cases, the slight weight difference between the two isn't a huge deal, but it's something to consider if you're optimizing your setup for low weight.
- Ease of Manufacturing: ABS is easier to mold and machine, which is why it's often used for RC car bodies and other parts where complex shapes are needed. ABS parts can also be painted easily, which makes it a common choice for body shells that require a glossy finish or custom designs. Nylon requires a bit more effort to mold due to its higher melting point and tendency to absorb moisture. It's also not as easy to paint as ABS. However, this doesn't stop it from being used in the more mechanical parts of the car where durability is the priority over aesthetics.
- Cost: ABS tends to be a bit cheaper to produce, especially for larger parts like body shells. Nylon, due to its toughness and more complex molding process, can be slightly more expensive in comparison, but it is often worth the extra cost for high-stress mechanical parts.

Nylon is generally better for parts that need to bend, flex, or withstand heavy impacts without breaking. It's ideal for suspension arms, gears, shock towers, and anything that needs to absorb shock or vibration. If you're doing a lot of off-roading or bashing, or if you're using your car for aggressive driving, nylon is the go-to material. In contrast, ABS is better for parts that need to be rigid and strong but don't need to flex. If you're looking for a lightweight, rigid body shell or some structural components in a car that will see a lot of on-road racing or low-impact conditions, ABS will be a better choice.

What about glass fiber-reinforced plastic? Glass fiber-reinforced plastic, often called GFRP, is a composite material where glass fibers are blended into a plastic matrix, usually nylon. This combination creates a material that is significantly stronger and stiffer than ordinary plastic, while remaining durable and resistant to cracking under heavy loads or impacts. In the world of RC cars, GFRP plays an important role, particularly in performance-focused designs. GFRP is frequently used for critical structural parts such as chassis decks, shock towers, suspension arms, and steering components. Compared to pure nylon or ABS, GFRP parts feel much harder and resist bending or twisting under stress, which leads to more stable suspension geometry and sharper, more responsive handling. The car behaves more precisely on the track because important components stay aligned better during hard driving. Although GFRP is heavier than full carbon fiber composites and slightly less stiff, it offers an excellent balance between cost, strength, and performance. This makes it a popular choice for mid-level and even some high-end RC race kits. For instance, Tamiya often uses GFRP in their TA and TRF series, and many aftermarket "carbon-reinforced" upgrade parts marketed for cars like the TT-02 or DF-03 are actually made from GFRP, not pure carbon fiber.

The importance of metal front knuckles

Changing your RC car's front knuckles from plastic to metal is mainly about making the car stronger and more reliable. Plastic knuckles, while light and cheap, are often the weak point in the steering system because they have to deal with all the forces from the wheels—especially during crashes, hard landings, or even just aggressive driving on rough surfaces. Over time, plastic gets worn out, stressed, or brittle, especially if the car is used a lot outdoors where temperature changes and dirt can weaken it. Metal knuckles, on the other hand, resist bending and snapping much better, giving you a tougher, longer-lasting part that can handle bigger impacts without failure.

Front knuckles usually break because they are under constant stress whenever the wheels turn, hit bumps, or land awkwardly. Every time you clip a curb, land from a jump with the wheels slightly turned, or even just roll over uneven terrain, you're putting a lot of force through the steering knuckles. Plastic can only flex so much before it cracks. Also, crashes often twist the front wheels sharply, which puts sudden, uneven loads on the knuckles and causes them to snap right at the pivot points or where the steering link attaches.

To avoid breaking your knuckles, there are a few smart habits you can adopt. First, try to drive a little smoother, especially when landing jumps—keeping the wheels straight during a landing can help a lot. Secondly, make sure the suspension is tuned well so it absorbs more impact instead of passing it all through the steering system. Regularly checking for worn bearings or loose parts can also prevent stress from building up in one weak spot. And if you know you're going to be pushing your RC hard—like big jumps, bashing over rocks, or racing—then upgrading to metal knuckles ahead of time is a smart move, because you'll be preventing the problem rather than fixing it after something breaks.

When the front knuckles keep breaking, it usually means the forces going into them are just a bit too much for the stock plastic to handle. It could be from the way the car is landing after jumps, from heavy wheels or tires, from steering hitting full lock during crashes, or even just from the material starting to get fatigued after a lot of use. Some plastics (especially cheaper ones) get a little brittle over time, especially if they've been exposed to cold weather or sunlight. Switching to metal knuckles is a very solid fix because they'll handle much more abuse without giving up. Some people also pair metal knuckles with stronger steering links and better hub carriers if they really want the front end bulletproof. Another thing that can quietly help is adjusting your steering end points on the transmitter—limiting maximum steering angle just a tiny bit can reduce the stress that twists and snaps the knuckles during a hard hit.

ESC failsafe

Under normal operation, the ESC receives a continuous signal from the receiver that reflects the throttle input from the transmitter. If this signal is lost—for example, if the transmitter is turned off, the receiver battery dies, or the car moves out of range—the ESC needs to know what to do. Without a fail-safe, the ESC might continue outputting the last known throttle signal, which could keep the motor running at speed, leading to dangerous situations or damage.

The most common ESC fail-safe behavior is to immediately reduce the throttle to zero or apply full braking. This stops or slows down the car as quickly as possible. Many modern ESCs allow you to program a specific fail-safe throttle setting. This might be neutral, full brake, or a controlled deceleration rate, depending on your application (e.g., off-road racing vs. crawling). Some ESCs even have a short delay (a fraction of a second) before activating fail-safe behavior to avoid triggering during brief signal glitches. Low-Voltage Cutoff Fail-Safe is special as it protects the battery (especially LiPo) by reducing or cutting throttle when voltage drops too low, preventing over-discharge.

Modern 2.4g transmitter features

Almost all modern RC car 2.4GHz transmitters now feature built-in displays for configuration settings because the complexity and expectations of RC systems have significantly evolved. These displays serve both functional and user experience purposes.

The main reason is convenience and control. RC systems today offer a wide range of programmable features—such as throttle curves, dual rates, exponential settings, ABS braking, servo reversing, endpoint adjustments, and model memory. Without a display, configuring these features would require cryptic button combinations or external setup tools, which is inefficient and error-prone. A screen allows users to easily view, adjust, and verify settings in a structured, menu-driven format.

Another key factor is model memory and flexibility. Many hobbyists use the same transmitter for multiple vehicles. The display enables quick switching between saved profiles, which streamlines setup when using different RC cars with different configurations. Additionally, modern transmitters are designed to appeal to a more tech-savvy, performance-focused audience. A screen improves user interface quality, making the transmitter feel more advanced and responsive—similar to what people expect from consumer electronics.

You would change the dual rate settings on your RC transmitter to adjust how much your steering (or sometimes throttle) responds to your input without changing the mechanical setup of the car itself. Dual rate is basically a way of limiting or expanding the maximum travel of the servo through the transmitter. You might particularly want to lower the dual rate if the steering feels too aggressive, twitchy, or sensitive, especially at high speeds. When you're going fast, even a small movement of the steering can make the car veer sharply, which makes it harder to drive smoothly. By dialing down the dual rate, you reduce how far the wheels turn for a given movement of the steering wheel or stick on your transmitter. This makes the car feel calmer, more stable, and easier to control. On the other hand, you might increase the dual rate if you need sharper, tighter steering, like when you're driving on a small, technical track or trying to make quick turns. In that case, you want the wheels to turn more aggressively with less input, so you turn the dual rate up and get the full mechanical steering range your car can handle.

Adjusting the dual rate is really about matching the car's response to the conditions you're driving in and the way you personally like to control the car. Fast, open spaces often call for lower dual rate for stability, while tight, twisty tracks or indoor racing might make you want more steering action. Sometimes people also change the dual rate mid-run if the surface grip changes, like from dry to wet, to keep the car feeling balanced and predictable.

Hobbywing ESCs

Everyone seems to be using Hobbywing ESCs in RC car racing because they've built a strong reputation for performance, reliability, and tunability that racers really trust. In competitive racing, consistency is everything — you can't afford weird glitches, overheating, or random failures — and Hobbywing has proven over time that their ESCs can take the heat (literally and figuratively) while staying smooth and predictable.

One huge reason is that Hobbywing ESCs have excellent throttle and brake control. Their firmware is really finely tuned, which means you get super smooth acceleration and very precise braking, and that gives racers a huge advantage when trying to shave off tenths of a second each lap. They also have a lot of adjustable settings, like punch control, drag brake strength, and boost/turbo timing, which lets drivers dial in exactly how the car behaves based on track conditions and their driving style. And despite all that tunability, the ESCs are still considered very user-friendly, with programming cards or apps that make changes quick and simple between heats.

Another factor is that Hobbywing supports both "blinky" spec racing and boosted modified racing with their ESCs. In spec racing (where everyone runs similar setups), it's critical to have an ESC that doesn't give hidden advantages or inconsistencies, and Hobbywing has always been seen as very fair and transparent in that area, which made race organizers and serious racers trust them even more. And finally, they're also priced really competitively compared to some other high-end brands. So for a lot of racers, it's a no-brainer: you get factory-level performance without having to spend crazy money, and you can race with confidence knowing your electronics won't be the reason you lose.

Throttle adjustment

With a modern ESC, throttle adjustment is typically done through one of three main methods: transmitter programming, a dedicated program card, or a digital interface like a USB link or smartphone app, depending on the ESC's brand and features.

The most common and basic way is via the transmitter, especially when first setting up the ESC. This process usually involves entering a calibration mode, where you power on the ESC with the throttle at full, then follow a sequence (full throttle, full brake, then neutral) so the ESC learns the full range of your transmitter's throttle positions. This ensures smooth and accurate throttle response.

For more detailed adjustments—like throttle curve, punch (initial acceleration), drag brake, or brake strength—many ESCs require a program card. These plug directly into the ESC and give you access to a menu of adjustable parameters. You can increase throttle sensitivity, set a linear or exponential throttle curve, or fine-tune how aggressively the ESC responds to trigger input.

Some advanced ESCs offer digital programming through a USB link or Bluetooth module, using a PC program or mobile app. These interfaces provide even finer control and sometimes graphical interfaces for throttle curves. They also allow for saving and switching between different profiles, which is useful if you run the same car in multiple environments.

So, in modern systems, you typically start with basic calibration using the transmitter, then use either a program card or digital tool to adjust the finer throttle settings based on your needs—whether for racing, crawling, bashing, or drifting.

ESC program card

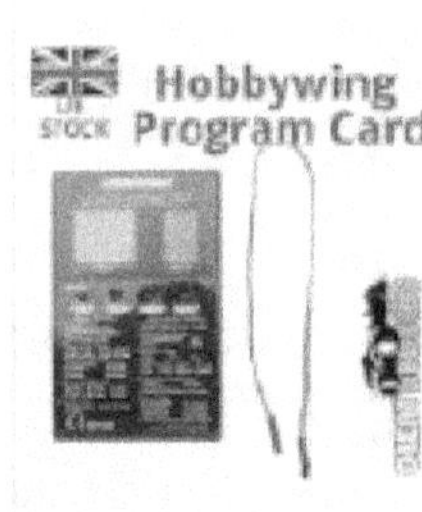

Hobbywing Led Program Card...	Hobbywing Hobbywing...	Hobbywing LED Program Card...	Hobbywing 30501003...	Hobbywing 120A LED Program...
£9.88	**£12.99**	**£9.88**	**£15.65**	**£3.69**
eBay	UK.Banggood	eBay.co.uk	Amazon.co.uk	Aliexpress
Free delivery	+£2.51 delivery	Free delivery	Free delivery	Free delivery
		★ ★ ★ ★ ★ (9)		★ ★ ★ ★ ★ (24)
By Shopping.com	By Google	By Stendia	By Kelkoo	By Mr.Shopping

An ESC program card is a handheld or small plug-in device used to configure the ESC settings. Instead of relying on complicated stick programming via the transmitter, which can be time-consuming and imprecise, a program card provides a user-friendly interface—usually with buttons and a screen or a series of LEDs—to adjust settings. These program cards are typically vendor-specific, not universal. Each ESC brand—and often each product line within a brand—uses its own firmware and communication protocols. This means a Hobbywing program card, for instance, usually only works with compatible Hobbywing ESCs. Some brands may have a bit more compatibility within their product ranges (e.g., an older card might work with several generations of ESCs), but generally, you can't use one brand's card to program a different brand's ESC.

There are a few exceptions: some generic ESCs or rebranded models share the same architecture and may work with the same card, especially if they are based on a common OEM design. However, unless you know for sure the ESCs are built on the same platform, it's safest to assume you must use the correct card for your ESC brand and model.

Using the right program card is essential not only to access the full range of settings but also to avoid communication errors or potential misconfiguration that could harm the ESC or motor. In some cases, manufacturers also offer USB links or Bluetooth modules as alternatives to program cards, allowing programming through a computer or smartphone app. But again, these tools are also vendor-specific.

ESC timing and Turbo mode

Timing in an ESC is all about how the ESC controls the phase timing of the motor's electrical signals to influence how the motor behaves — particularly its speed, torque, and efficiency. In simple terms, timing is like adjusting when the motor's magnetic fields "fire" relative to the position of the motor's rotor. If you advance the timing (meaning you fire the magnets a little earlier), you can make the motor spin faster and produce more top-end power. This is really useful for tracks where you need more straight-line speed. However, increasing timing also makes the motor run hotter and less efficient, because you're working it harder and creating more internal friction and electrical loss. On the flip side, if you reduce timing (retard the timing), the motor will run cooler, have more torque at low speeds, and be more efficient, but it won't be as fast at the top end. Low timing is often better for technical tracks where you need more control and less heat buildup, or when you're trying to make your battery last longer during a race.

ESC timing can be fixed (like in "blinky" mode where there is no added timing at all) or dynamic (like with "boost" and "turbo" settings). Boost adds timing progressively as motor RPMs rise, and turbo gives a big shot of timing once a certain RPM or throttle position is hit. Racers use these features to get acceleration and top speed advantages without sacrificing too much low-end drivability. After all, managing timing is a balancing act. Too much timing and your motor might overheat, wear out faster, or even damage itself. Too little and your car might be sluggish compared to the competition. Getting it right is part of fine-tuning your car to match the track, weather conditions, and your driving style.

Only sensored brushless motors can run in turbo mode — and this is by design. Turbo mode allows the ESC to dynamically advance motor timing at high RPMs to increase power and speed. This can give a significant performance boost on straightaways, where extra timing can be safely applied without overheating the motor. The key reason turbo mode requires a sensored motor is that this feature relies on precise rotor position feedback from the motor's sensors. That real-time data lets the ESC accurately control timing changes across the RPM range. Without sensors, the ESC can't reliably detect the rotor's position or speed at low RPMs, and certainly not accurately enough to apply timing dynamically at high speeds. Trying to run turbo mode on a sensorless system would lead to unpredictable behavior and could easily overheat or damage the motor.

Sensorless systems estimate position based on back-EMF (voltage feedback from the motor), but this only becomes reliable after the motor is already spinning. That's why sensorless ESCs can't support fine-grained timing controls like boost or turbo, which are applied in relation to exact rotor position and RPM.

Balance mode charging

Charging a LiPo battery in balanced mode means that the charger monitors and attempts to equalize the voltage of each individual cell during the charging process. However, even when the charger reports that the battery is fully charged and balanced, the cells are often not truly or perfectly balanced. This discrepancy arises from several factors related to how chargers function, how batteries behave, and the limitations of the balancing process itself.

Most hobby-grade LiPo chargers rely on a passive balancing method, which discharges higher-voltage cells through small resistors to bring them down to match the lower-voltage cells. This process is inherently slow, with balancing currents typically in the range of 50 to 300 milliamps. If the cells in the pack are significantly out of balance, the charger may not have enough time—or capacity—to bring them into precise alignment before it concludes the charge cycle, especially if the balancing circuitry cannot keep up with the main charging current. Many chargers will terminate the process when either the total pack voltage reaches the set point or the current falls below a cutoff threshold, even if small differences still exist between the cells.

Additionally, the balancing circuitry operates within a certain voltage tolerance—usually around ±0.01 to 0.05 volts. As a result, the charger may consider the pack "balanced" even if there is a noticeable difference between cells, such as one being at 4.20 volts while another is at 4.17. While this difference might seem small, repeated cycling under these conditions can cause the imbalance to worsen over time, leading to performance loss or even cell damage in extreme cases.

Battery aging also plays a role. Over time, the individual cells in a pack may degrade at different rates due to variations in internal resistance, thermal exposure, or mechanical stress. This leads to one or more cells charging or discharging slightly faster or slower than the others, making it increasingly difficult for the charger to equalize them fully within a single session. Furthermore, if the balance lead connectors are dirty, corroded, or loose, the charger may not be able to read cell voltages accurately or apply balancing corrections effectively.

A LiPo battery checker is a device specifically designed to read the voltage of each cell in a LiPo pack. It's easy to use and provides quick and accurate readings. Some advanced models also display the overall health of the battery, internal resistance, and voltage differences between cells. You simply plug the balance leads into the corresponding input on the battery checker. It should display the individual cell voltages. The display will usually show something like Cell 1, Cell 2, and so on. It will also show the overall pack voltage and sometimes the voltage difference between cells, which is helpful for determining imbalance. If cells are imbalanced consistently by more than 0.05V, you may want to balance the pack using a balancer charger that can perform a more thorough balancing process. Alternatively, you can try to balance the cells manually if your charger allows for that. If there's a significant voltage difference (e.g., 0.1V or more) between cells over several cycles, it could indicate an issue with one or more cells that may need to be addressed by replacing the pack or performing further diagnosis.

Safe charging current

The safe charging current for most 2S LiPo batteries is typically 1C, which means charging at a current equal to the battery's capacity. For example, if your 2S LiPo has a capacity of 3500mAh (or 3.5Ah), a 1C charge rate would be 3.5 amps.

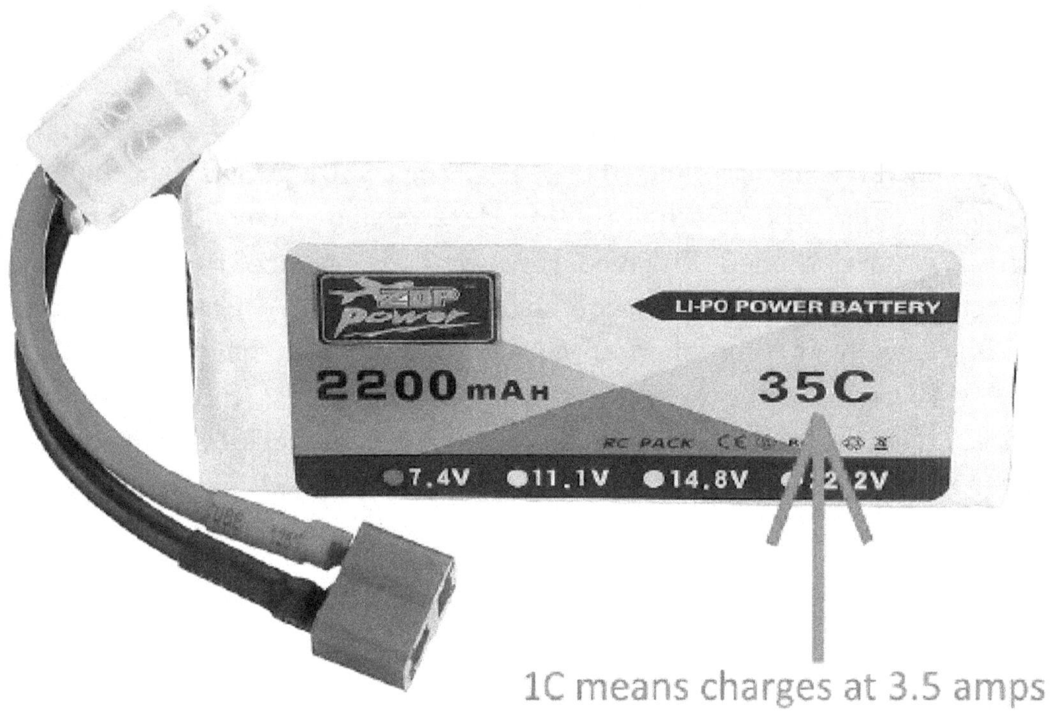

Charging at 1C is considered the industry standard because it balances safety, battery longevity, and convenience. It keeps heat buildup minimal and helps ensure the battery lasts through many charge cycles without swelling or losing capacity prematurely.

Some modern LiPos are rated for higher charge rates, such as 2C, 3C, or even more, which would allow you to charge faster (e.g., 10A for a 5000mAh pack at 2C). However, you should only charge above 1C if the manufacturer explicitly states it's safe. Otherwise, sticking to 1C is the safest and most conservative option.

Rescuing a nearly dead LiPo

Rescuing a nearly dead LiPo battery is a risky process that should only be attempted under very specific conditions. A LiPo is considered nearly dead when the voltage of any of its cells drops below 3.0 volts, and especially if it falls under 2.5 volts. At that stage, most smart chargers will refuse to begin a standard LiPo charge cycle. Before trying to revive the battery, it's absolutely essential to confirm that the pack is not swollen, physically damaged, or leaking. If any of those signs are present, the battery is unsafe and must be disposed of properly at a battery recycling center.

If the battery appears physically intact and the only issue is that its voltage is too low, some users attempt a cautious workaround. One common method involves using a charger with a NiMH or NiCd mode, since those charging profiles do not rely on minimum voltage detection like LiPo modes do. By trickle charging the battery at a very low current—typically between 0.1 and 0.5 amps—it's sometimes possible to raise the cell voltages just high enough for the charger to once again recognize it as a LiPo pack. However, this step must be done with extreme care. The battery should never be left unattended during this phase, and the voltage must be monitored closely. As soon as each cell rises above roughly 3.2 volts, the charging should be stopped immediately. Once the voltage has been safely raised above the cutoff point, the battery can then be switched back to the charger's standard LiPo balance charging mode. At that point, it should be charged slowly—ideally at a lower-than-normal current such as 0.5 to 1.0 amps—until it reaches full voltage. Even if this process succeeds, it doesn't guarantee that the battery is safe or reliable. A recovered LiPo may no longer hold a charge properly, may become unbalanced quickly, or may degrade under load. It should never be used again in high-demand scenarios like racing or aggressive off-roading. Instead, it might be relegated to light-duty use or simply discarded if performance remains poor. If, after attempting recovery, the battery continues to show signs of trouble—such as unbalanced cells, rapid voltage drop, heating during charging, or puffing—it should be considered unsafe. In that case, the only responsible action is to retire it and dispose of it at an appropriate recycling facility. Recovery can sometimes work in mild cases of over-discharge, but it's not a guaranteed fix, and the risks involved mean that many experienced hobbyists simply choose to replace the battery rather than take the chance of fire or failure.

Why is LiFE not popular?

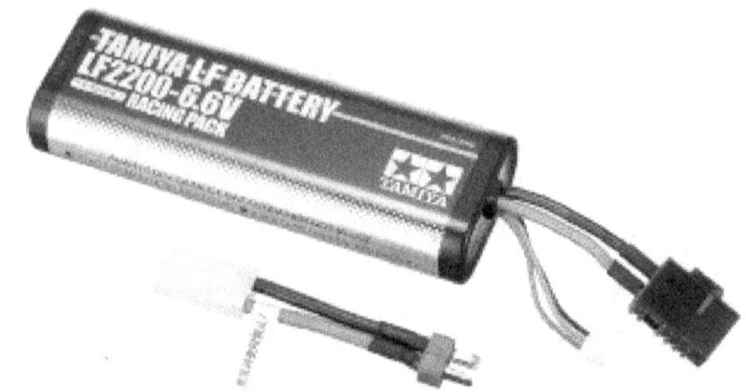

LiFe (Lithium Iron Phosphate) batteries are less popular than LiPo batteries in the RC world mainly because they trade off performance for safety and longevity, and most RC users prioritize power, size, and weight over those other benefits. The biggest reason LiPos dominate is their higher energy density. For the same size and weight, a LiPo can store more energy and deliver higher voltage, which directly translates to faster speeds and more powerful acceleration—critical for performance-focused RC cars, drones, and aircraft. LiPos also typically offer higher discharge rates (C-ratings), making them better suited for the short, intense bursts of power required in racing and bashing.

LiFe batteries, by comparison, have a lower nominal voltage (around 3.3V per cell versus 3.7V for LiPo), which means a 2S LiFe pack delivers 6.6V versus 7.4V from a 2S LiPo. That lower voltage results in noticeably reduced speed and punch unless you compensate with extra cells or gearing changes, which can add weight or complexity. Additionally, LiFe packs tend to be bulkier for the same capacity, making them harder to fit into the tight battery trays of many RC models.

However, LiFe batteries do have clear advantages in safety and cycle life. They're much more stable chemically, far less prone to catching fire or swelling, and they can handle hundreds more charge cycles than LiPos. They're also more tolerant of abuse, such as overcharging or deep discharging. Because of this, LiFe batteries are sometimes used in transmitter packs, receiver packs, or robotics—where reliability and safety matter more than raw performance.

Despite those strengths, most hobbyists still choose LiPo because the performance gains are so noticeable and necessary in competitive or high-speed applications. In essence, LiPo batteries are more popular because they offer more power, better performance, and a higher energy-to-weight ratio—three things that matter most in mainstream RC use, even if it means sacrificing a bit of safety and long-term durability.

What are the modern alternatives to deans plug?

Modern alternatives to the Deans plug (also known as T-plug) have become increasingly popular due to improvements in current handling, ease of use, safety, and durability. While Deans connectors were once the go-to standard for many RC applications, several other connectors now dominate the scene depending on power level and user preference.

One of the most widely adopted alternatives is the XT60 connector. It's favored for its secure fit, ability to handle high current (up to 60A continuous), and ease of soldering. XT60 connectors are also polarized, preventing reverse polarity, and have become a standard in many RC planes, drones, and cars. For higher current applications, the XT90 and XT150 connectors offer even more capacity.

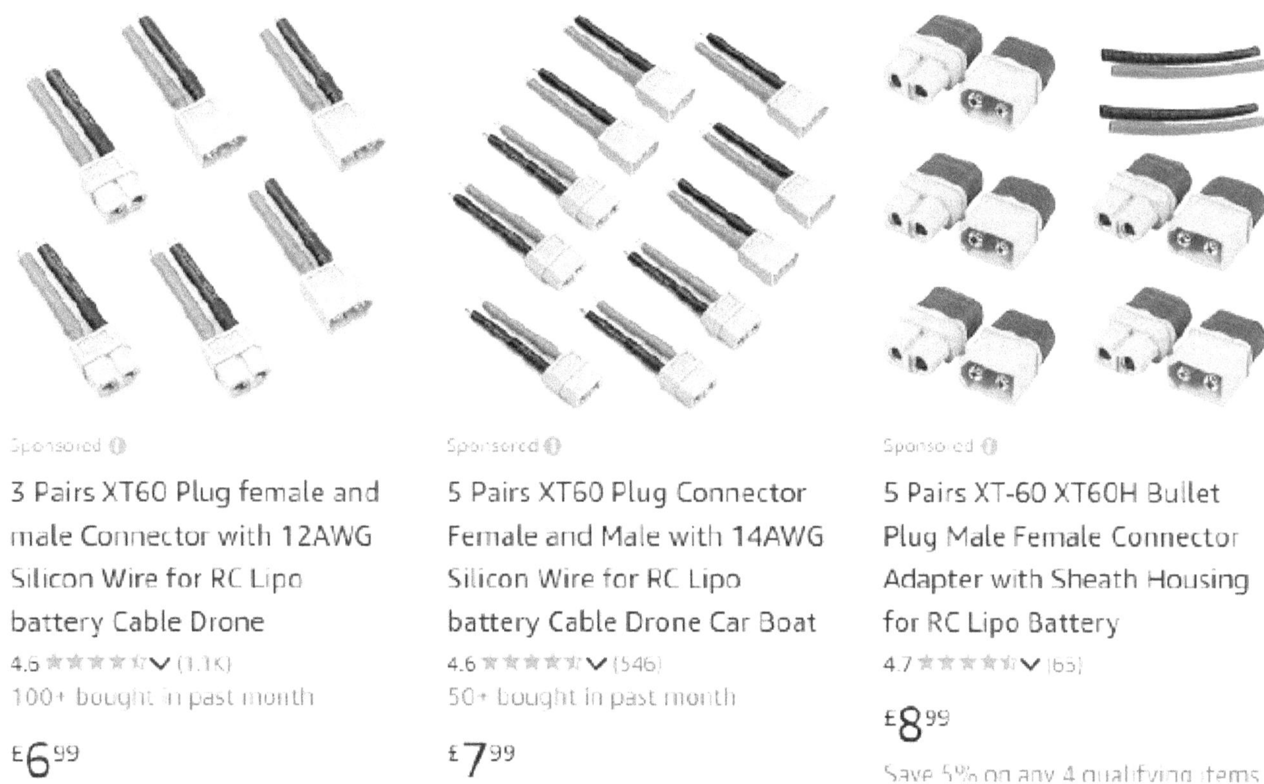

3 Pairs XT60 Plug female and male Connector with 12AWG Silicon Wire for RC Lipo battery Cable Drone

4.6 ★★★★☆ (1.1K)
100+ bought in past month

£6⁹⁹

5 Pairs XT60 Plug Connector Female and Male with 14AWG Silicon Wire for RC Lipo battery Cable Drone Car Boat

4.6 ★★★★☆ (546)
50+ bought in past month

£7⁹⁹

5 Pairs XT-60 XT60H Bullet Plug Male Female Connector Adapter with Sheath Housing for RC Lipo Battery

4.7 ★★★★☆ (63)

£8⁹⁹

Save 5% on any 4 qualifying items

Another popular option is the EC3 and EC5 series from E-flite and Horizon Hobby. EC3 connectors handle about 60A, while EC5s can manage 120A or more. They are known for their robust build and are often used in larger RC vehicles and aircraft. Like XT connectors, EC connectors are also polarized and provide a solid connection.

The AS150 connector is sometimes seen in high-voltage applications (such as 8S or 12S LiPo setups), especially in large-scale RC planes and electric bikes, where safe high-current delivery is essential.

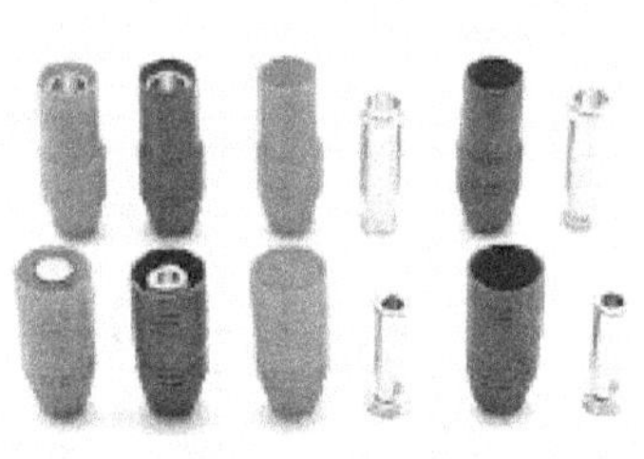

IC connectors (like IC3 and IC5), which are backward-compatible with EC3 and EC5, add the benefit of built-in smart technology when used with Spektrum Smart ESCs and batteries. These allow data transmission between battery and ESC, offering information like voltage, capacity, temperature, and charge cycles.

What is the primary difference between 1/8 offroad and 1/10 offroad?

The primary difference between 1/8 and 1/10 scale off-road RC vehicles is their size and power, which directly affects durability, performance, and the type of terrain they can handle.

A 1/8 scale off-road RC car is significantly larger, heavier, and more powerful than its 1/10 counterpart. These vehicles are built for extreme off-road conditions and high-speed bashing or racing. They usually feature more robust drivetrains, larger tires, stronger suspension components, and higher voltage power systems—commonly running on 4S or 6S LiPo batteries with powerful brushless motors. Because of their size and power, they can tackle rougher terrain, larger jumps, and more demanding race tracks. They're also typically more expensive and require more space for use and storage.

In contrast, a 1/10 scale off-road vehicle is smaller, lighter, and generally more affordable. These cars often run on 2S or 3S LiPo setups and are well-suited for backyard driving, indoor tracks, or lighter off-road use like dirt trails or gravel. While still capable, they can be less forgiving over large jumps or extremely rough terrain due to their lower ground clearance and less rugged components. However, they're more portable, easier to work on in tight spaces, and more beginner-friendly in terms of cost and manageability.

In essence, 1/8 off-road vehicles offer more performance and durability for extreme use, while 1/10 vehicles provide greater accessibility, lower cost, and suitability for moderate off-road conditions. Your choice depends largely on your driving environment, experience level, and budget.

When would you opt for 4S or 5S for offroad RC?

Choosing between 4S and 5S LiPo batteries for an off-road RC setup depends on several key factors: the vehicle's size and weight, the terrain you're running on, your ESC and motor specs, and the kind of driving experience you want—whether it's speed, torque, or runtime.

You would typically go for 4S power if you're running a 1/8 scale off-road RC car, like a truggy or buggy, and you want a strong balance of speed, control, and reliability. 4S (14.8V) is a common sweet spot for powerful bashing and racing. It delivers a significant jump in torque and speed over 3S, without stressing your drivetrain as much as 6S. Many RTR 1/8 buggies are tuned for 4S, making it a safe and effective choice. It's ideal for rough terrain, big jumps, and fast-paced off-road tracks, especially if you want performance without excessive wear or thermal issues.

You'd consider 5S (18.5V) when you're looking for more punch and top-end speed than 4S, but you're not quite ready to jump to 6S, which can be brutal on components. 5S offers a kind of middle ground—it's less common and often used by more experienced hobbyists who custom-tune their vehicles. You might go for 5S if you're running a custom-built rig, a heavier 1/8 scale basher, or a truck that needs a bit more voltage to really shine—like when tackling deep grass, sand, or loose dirt at high speed. However, not all ESCs or motors are rated for 5S, so you'd need to check your electronics carefully before committing.

In short, choose 4S if you want strong, reliable performance and wide compatibility with 1/8 scale setups. Consider 5S if you're looking to push the limits with extra power but still want to avoid the full stress of 6S—assuming your hardware can handle it.

Thank you for reading. More RC books to come. For the latest updates please visit our website:

http://rcpress.com

To learn more about 3d printing of RC parts, please visit

http://UpgradePARTS.com

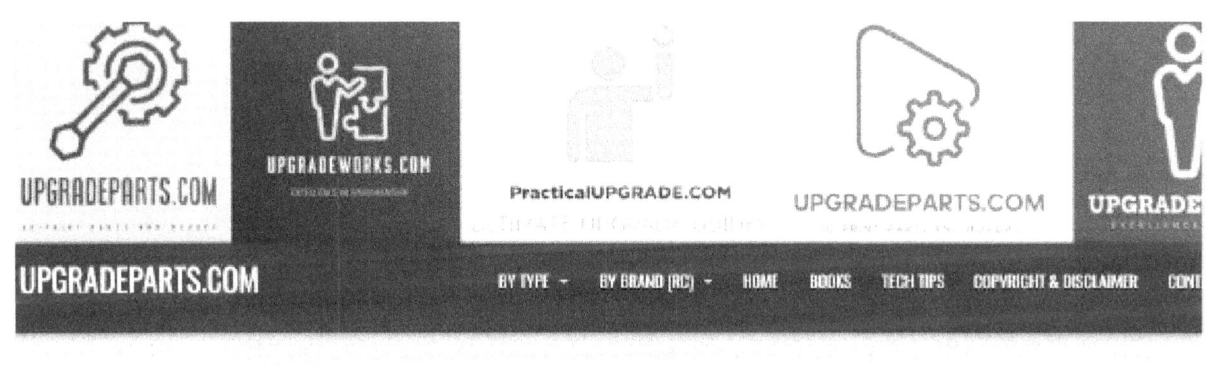

TT01 shock mount replacement

Version 1: This is a shock mount replacement for TT01 (normal) upgradeparts-tami-tt01-shockmount-replace Version 2: This is a shock mount

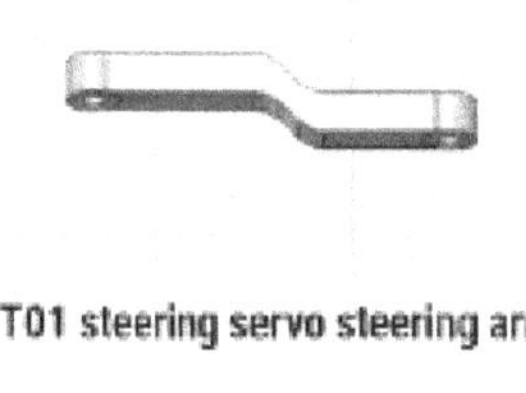

TT01 steering servo steering arm

TT01 steering servo steering arm, upgradeparts-tami-tt01-servosteering_arm